The Jossey-Bass
Higher and Adult Education Series

# Rethinking Student Affairs Practice

Patrick G. Love
Sandra M. Estanek

JOSSEY-BASS
A Wiley Imprint
www.josseybass.com

Published by Jossey-Bass
A Wiley Imprint
989 Market Street, San Francisco, CA 94103-1741   www.josseybass.com

Jossey-Bass books and products are available through most bookstores. To contact Jossey-Bass directly call our Customer Care Department within the U.S. at 800-956-7739, outside the U.S. at 317-572-3986 or fax 317-572-4002.

Jossey-Bass also publishes its books in a variety of electronic formats. Some content that appears in print may not be available in electronic books.

**Library of Congress Cataloging-in-Publication Data**

Love, Patrick.
  Rethinking student affairs practice / Patrick G. Love, Sandra M. Estanek.— 1st ed.
      p. cm. — (The Jossey-Bass higher and adult education series)
  Includes bibliographical references and index.
  ISBN 0-7879-6214-7 (alk. paper)
  1.  Student affairs services—United States. 2.  Student affairs administrators—United States.  I. Estanek, Sandra M. II. Title. III. Series.
  LB2342.92.L68 2004
  378.1'94'0973—dc22
                                    2003027458

Printed in the United States of America
FIRST EDITION

*HB Printing*          10 9 8 7 6 5 4 3 2 1

# Contents

*From Patrick*
*I dedicate this book to Anne, Conor, and Garrett—the Home*
*Team, and to the hundreds of students throughout my faculty life*
*who have caused me to rethink my student affairs practice.*

*From Sandra*
*I dedicate this book to my late parents, Bob and Mary Estanek,*
*who worked so hard to provide an education for my brother and*
*me, and to all of the dedicated student affairs professionals with*
*whom I have had the pleasure to have worked.*

# Preface

This book is about seeing things differently. Seeing differently is the ability to perceive our responsibilities, our institutions, and our relationships through multiple filters and frameworks. Seeing differently is reflecting on our current situations and discerning new possibilities inherent in them. Seeing differently is what philosophers have called dialectical thinking. To think dialectically is to reflect upon one's current situation in order to see new potential inherent in that situation. Change that is dialectical can succeed because it is grounded in the present while projecting into the future. It is based upon concrete analysis as well as creative imagination. Dialectical thinking is not utopian. It does not argue "this is the way it should be" and then create an alternative vision as the basis for change. Change that is based upon utopian thinking often fails.

In this book we advocate changing how we do the work of student affairs by learning how to think differently. As professionals learn to do this they may see the need to do some new and different things. Some of the things done now, when viewed through a different perspective, will be seen as less important or less effective than previously believed, and therefore they may be done in different ways or even cease being done altogether.

Let us illustrate with an example of what we mean by thinking differently. Think of those old foreground-background illusions: is it a fountain or two people about to kiss? Is it Freud or a beautiful

A Rabbit...or a Duck?
Hint: The duck is looking left,
the rabbit is looking right

woman? Is it a rabbit or a duck? In these puzzles both images cannot be seen at the same time, because each is the context for the
other. If they are both being seen, then neither image is being seen.
A new object is seen. One image needs to be the context for the
other in order for the viewer to see the other image and vice versa.
But both images are there. They are both foreground and background, but not at the same time.

The other important aspect of this illustration is that the image
itself does not change at all! It is the perspective and perception of
the viewer that changes. We influence what we see. This is what is
meant by seeing differently. This exercise demonstrates that individuals determine what is seen within the context of multiple possibilities. In a given situation there are multiple ways of seeing and
understanding. Often the tendency is to believe the one possibility
seen first is the only way to understand the picture, and this is acted
upon. Yes, it is a duck! Alternative understandings are not often
explored and, thus, the possibility of a new synthesis is missed. In
this book the reader will be asked to look for the rabbit if she or he
sees the duck, and to look for the duck if she or he sees the rabbit.
The challenge is to think differently, to think dialectically.

When we began this project we knew encouraging student affairs
professionals to think differently is what we wanted to do. We
wanted readers to think differently about the work of student affairs,
but we wanted to do so in a way that was not utopian. We wanted
to produce a work that was useful to student affairs practitioners in

the field while also challenging many current ways of thinking and doing. We knew where we wanted to go but we were not sure how to get there when we began. Like everyone who begins a project like this we began to "read around." We read outside the literature of student affairs and higher education. We read organizational behavior and leadership literature. We read political science and business. We were looking for a conceptual framework that would help us tie this book together and help us get where we knew we wanted to go.

We found that framework in the work of the "new science;" including quantum physics, chaos theory, and complexity theory. These sciences describe a universe that is infinitely complex and constantly changing. We were struck by the writings of authors who applied this new science to organizational behavior and leadership. These authors, particularly Margaret Wheatley and Danah Zohar, used the insights of the new science to ask businesspeople to approach organizational complexity and change differently. We came to believe that a framework informed by this perspective could help student affairs practitioners think of their work in new ways as well. The four interrelated elements of our conceptual schema taken from the insights of the new science are valuing dualisms, transcending paradigms, recognizing connectedness, and embracing paradox, which we introduce in the first chapter along with the work of Wheatley and Zohar. But before moving to that, we first address why we believe it is important to see the work of student affairs differently.

There is no question that institutions of higher education, regardless of their size, are complex and changing organizations. As student affairs has tried to meet the needs of more diverse people it has become more diverse and complex. That is the duck. But as individual professionals we have become specialists. That is the rabbit. To make the diversity and complexity of the organization more manageable, the work has been broken into digestible pieces. Responsibilities have been divided up. In this process professionals have become focused on and expert in those things that are his or her responsibility. This specialization is often referred to as the "silo structure" of higher education. This specialized focus makes it more difficult to avoid silo thinking, seeing the situation only from the point of view of one's own specialization.

We are not the first to recognize this dynamic of complexity and specialization in the university in general and in student affairs in particular. A reading of the 1949 version of "A Student Personnel Point of View" (American Council on Education, 1949/1994) demonstrates that even while calling for the establishment of student affairs as a separate profession, the writers of this document cautioned practitioners not to lose the holistic approach to their work with students.

Student affairs professionals continue to wrestle with this tension between holistic philosophy and divided administrative structures today as they did in 1949. Contemporary statements of the philosophy of student affairs reflect both the commitment to the whole student and the reality of the "functional silos" of academic bureaucracy. For example, the Student Learning Imperative states, "Student affairs professionals attempt to make 'seamless' what are often perceived by students to be disjointed, unconnected experiences by bridging organizational boundaries and forging collaborative partnerships with faculty and others to enhance student learning" (Schroeder, 1996, p. 120). Also, one of the "principles of good practice" that emerged from the Student Learning Imperative is that student affairs forges educational partnerships that advance student learning (Blimling & Whitt, 1999). Blimling and Whitt (1999) write: "Collaboration does not come easily or naturally owing to the personalities, history, expertise, and territories that define colleges and universities. What is more remarkable is that collaboration does occur. What makes it possible is a common desire to do good for students. Few serve in a university who do not care about students" (p. 18).

The tendency toward specialization has become dominant. Our experience as administrators affirms this, as does our experience as preparation program faculty. We have noticed that it does not take our graduate students long to develop this kind of silo thinking. They believe in the education of the whole student, but soon focus exclusively on their piece of that whole. They soon can only see the duck. Sometimes they learn this directly from internship or assistantship supervisors, but more often they just pick it up because it is the world in which they practice their profession.

At the same time we recognize silo structures and silo thinking as part of the experience of student affairs professionals, we also recognize that there are efforts on campus to overcome silo structures and silo thinking. The need for collaboration between student affairs and academic affairs has been a major theme for the past decade. At some colleges and universities, initiatives such as freshman interest groups and other forms of learning communities have created such seamless environments for students (Love & Goodsell Love, 1995; Schuh & Whitt, 1999). Service learning projects connected with specific courses also attempt to connect students' in-class and out-of-class learning. And recently, there have been increasing instances of organizational restructuring whereby a formerly independent division of student affairs, typically reporting directly to the president, has become part of academic affairs, reporting to the provost. The rationale for this restructuring is that it removes the organizational barriers to collaboration between academic affairs and student affairs.

But Larrey (2002) argues that "organizational redesign has only modest impact in changing attitudes" (p. 105). Writing from the point of view of a provost, he argues there are three reasons this move to integrate student affairs into academic affairs will not produce the desired outcome and may in fact be detrimental to the role typically played in the university by student affairs. First, no significant theoretical groundwork has been laid for this new administrative structure. Second, old attitudes remain intact so transformation cannot be affected by the new organization, and third, the new model creates institutional imbalance by creating a "super-sized" division of academic affairs. Larrey understands real change is about thinking as much as it is about structure. For a new model to succeed, everyone must envision their work anew, and this typically has not occurred. If academic affairs sees the duck and student affairs sees the rabbit, both areas must begin to see the new image if restructuring is to be transformational. We agree with Larrey that attitudes must change and that we must articulate a new way of thinking about education if we want these organizational changes to have the desired effect. We have taken up his challenge in this book to articulate such a new way of thinking.

## Organization of the Book

In the first chapter we introduce the concepts of the "new science" and how those concepts have been applied to management by Margaret Wheatley, Danah Zohar, and others. We explain in this first chapter why we believe the insights of this literature are applicable to higher education and the work of student affairs. Some may question the applicability of management literature to student affairs. Birnbaum (2001) has documented the progression of what he calls "management fads" in higher education. Many of these fads have come from business literature and have been applied on campuses under the direction of executive management. As Birnbaum states, and as our experience confirms, "Businesspeople are disproportionately represented on boards of trustees and are more likely than academics to think that running a college is like running a business" (p. 148). His argument is that the succession of these fads, such as total quality management (TQM), management by objectives (MBO), zero based budgeting, and benchmarking, have not succeeded in making higher education more efficient and effective. He challenges higher education professionals to approach new management ideas with "skeptical curiosity" (p. 231).

We are not proposing a new management fad. We are not suggesting that the new science provides a proven pathway to effectiveness and efficiency. One of the reasons reading Wheatley and Zohar resonated with our experience is they challenged precisely the types of management fads Birnbaum discusses, and they did so from within the framework of business itself. Those management strategies are about control. If the organization does X then Y will happen. As will be seen, the insight of the new science is that the world does not work this way. This literature helped us ask ourselves new questions and see new connections and possibilities. We agree with Birnbaum that readers should approach our ideas, arguments, and assertions with skeptical curiosity. We hope that readers will find what we say useful to their own creative thinking.

Something that frustrates us as former practitioners is to read literature that exhorts us to do new and different things but does not recognize the reality and constraints of the institutions in which we work. In this book we have tried to avoid this trap by focusing on how it is possible to think differently but within the context of one's current institutional structure. Subsequently, we have clustered the chapters into several broad parts. In Part One we discuss processes, in other words, the "how" we do our work, and in Part Two we discuss resources or the "what" with which we have to work. We conclude the book with three chapters in Part Three on emergent competencies.

Included in Part One dealing with processes are chapters on pervasive leadership, intrapreneurship, and developing an assessment mindset. Chapter Two is entitled "Pervasive Leadership," which says something of our perspective. Leadership can and should be exercised by all members of the community. It should be pervasive throughout the organization. The chapter on leadership is at the beginning of this book both physically and conceptually because in many ways the entire book is about pervasive leadership. We begin the chapter on pervasive leadership with a discussion of politics because we understand that being able to understand institutional politics is a necessary component of leadership. Rogers writes, "Politics is often a dirty word, especially among the helping professions.

Yet humans are political animals, and an understanding of the political process is essential in order to enact change" (1995, p. 314).

Chapter Three, "Intrapreneurship: Pervasive Leadership in Action," describes a process whereby the perspectives of pervasive leadership and the competencies of entrepreneurship are applied within the context of the organization.

Assessment, like politics, is also a topic that is viewed by many professionals as a necessary evil. It is often seen as additional work, required by those who do not understand student affairs and taking time away from working with students and other, more important tasks. Assessment is often done in order to fulfill the expectations of others and to justify the work of student affairs. No wonder few people like to do it! Again, we take a more positive and proactive view by understanding assessment as a process rather than just as a task. In Chapter Four, "Developing an Assessment Mindset," we discuss the perspective of assessment as a process of individual growth and organizational self-renewal. Assessment may still be required by regulation or for accreditation but thinking differently about the process can result in a different focus and be more useful and creative.

The focus of the book shifts to resources in Part Two. Obtaining and managing resources are understood as important skills for student affairs professionals to develop. But this again is often tinged with a negative perspective. Schuh (1990) writes, "A few years ago I observed that 'this is not a pleasant time to be responsible for financial institutions of higher education'" (p. 1). "If any improvements have occurred in the financial circumstances of higher education since then, the changes have been only marginally positive" (Schuh, 1996, p. 458). Schuh writes again, "This is not an easy time to be a budget officer or financial manager in an institution of higher education" (2000, p. 73). In these works and others, graduate students and young professionals are given the impression that money once flowed to student affairs but is no longer the case. They are told they have to do more and much of what they have to do is mandated by others; however, they will receive fewer resources to accomplish the tasks expected of them. Again, we take a more positive and proactive view. In Chapter Five, "Rethinking Resources," we discuss how resources can be reperceived and creatively generated in a context characterized by pervasive leadership and intrapreneurship.

In Chapter Six, "Technology as Brush, Paint, and Artist," we start from the perspective that technology is a tool, a skill, and a medium to be shaped. Going fast are the days when "techies" deliver hardware and software to departments, programs, and divisions and tell staff how to use them. The sophistication of technology has reached a point where it can be shaped to meet the needs and expectations of end users. It is time for student affairs to develop a philosophy of technology and to participate in shaping the technologies of the future.

In Part Three we present competencies that are just emerging on the horizon. Chapter Seven focuses on adopting a global perspective. Even before September 11, the war on terror, and the wars in Afghanistan and Iraq, events had progressed to the point where the ability to view the United States and American higher education as closed systems was in doubt. We argue in Chapter Seven for embracing a perspective that recognizes American higher education in a world context.

Finally, futures forecasting is a way of considering the future in a world that recognizes predictability as the fallacy it is. Chapter Eight argues student affairs professionals must work to influence and shape the future they are moving toward, and leads to the conclusions presented in Chapter Nine.

## About the Authors: A Community of Authorship in an Ongoing Dialogue

Working on this project has taught us to think differently in several ways. One of these is the way we have come to think about the book itself. We have come to understand the book as a moment in an ongoing dialogue within a community of authorship. Let us explain what we mean and why we think it is important to approach the book in that way.

On one level, of course, the book has two authors, Patrick G. Love and Sandra M. Estanek. Patrick Love is an associate professor in the student affairs master's and higher education doctoral program at New York University. He has been a faculty member for more than ten years and is a former student affairs administrator with experience in residence life, student activities, judicial affairs, and general administration. He now spends much of his time learning from and helping to prepare cadres of new professionals.

Sandra Estanek is an assistant professor and director of the student affairs master's program at Canisius College in Buffalo, New York. Sandy is new to the faculty ranks. She began her new life as a student affairs preparation program faculty member during the writing of this book and after a twenty-three-year career as a student affairs administrator, including the last fifteen years as a senior student affairs officer.

This book began in dialogue within a group of potential authors, from which emerged the two of us. We have known each other for several years and have worked on other projects together. Working to integrate theory and practice is something present in both of our careers and in the conversations we have had. It is something we wanted to make present in this work as well. With this book we wanted to write something to stretch the profession but we also wanted to write something practical that student affairs professionals working in the field could actually use.

The dialogue that is this book continued with a group of graduate students, some of whom have been with us since the beginning. This team of students was the first "audience" to engage with us and the ideas with which we were struggling. Samantha Buhr and Kristin Wodarski, the team captains, provided support, responsiveness, and leadership throughout the process. Kim Yousey, Terri Gurrieri, Jeff Spain, and John Gallagher researched and reviewed sources. They also challenged our thinking from the perspective of people who are new to the field of student affairs and who were potential target customers for such a volume. Sarah Schoper and Steve Hubbard read and responded to early messy drafts and provided critical feedback. Finally, there is Sara Bleiberg, who had the unenviable task of reading the first full draft of the book manuscript. Thanks to them and thanks to you for heading out on this journey with us.

You are the third member of this community of authorship. It is our intention to use the process of writing and publishing this book as a means of continuing to engage others in these ideas in an active way. The book does not exist only on paper; it exists in the relationships between you, your thoughts, your opinions and your experiences, and ours. This is not a new insight on our part. Biblical criticism, literary criticism, phenomenology, and deconstruction have long understood that the "text" includes all of these dimensions. But we have taken this insight another step. To consciously facilitate this dialogue of the text, we have created a Web site at www.rethinking-student-affairs-practice.com. In doing this project we were committed to challenging ourselves to think in nontraditional ways and to work in new ways, too. We gave ourselves the task of overcoming some of the dualisms that characterize our professional lives: theory and practice, practitioner and faculty, teacher and student, author and reader. We believe that by creating a Web site related to this book we can use technology to continue the dialogue we have begun. You know how it is. You buy a book, read it (or only get part way through it), and put it down. Sometimes you find something useful in it and perhaps you even incorporate some of it into your work. Sometimes you find something you wish to challenge or develop in new ways. In each case you wish you could talk to the book and not just about it. But the book is silent. It has said what it had to say. It exists as a whole, as something complete. It cannot participate in further dialogue with you.

But we have come to understand that it can! This book is not complete. We want the dialogue to continue and to be part of it with you. So we invite you to visit our Web site at any point in your reading, introduce yourself, and join the conversation.

## Acknowledgments

We have many people to thank for helping with this book, both in the actual research and writing and in the development of the ideas that form its foundation. First of all, the idea for this book grew out of a chapter, "Competencies and Perspectives for the New Millennium," in the monograph *Leadership and Management Issues for a New Century* that Patrick wrote with Doug Woodard and Susan Komives. The experience and conversations of that project provided the confidence and motivation to continue to develop and expand the ideas from that chapter. This is also an opportunity for Patrick to publicly thank Susan, because if it were not for a keynote speech she gave back in 1983, Patrick today would not be in the field of student affairs!

Other people assisted along the way, including Kathleen Manning, who was part of the initial team that developed the vision for this volume. In the text many of the students at New York University who helped are specified; however, we also wish to specifically acknowledge the work of Samantha Buhr and Kristin Wodarski, team captains and among the best master's students Patrick has had the pleasure of working with.

Those who assisted Sandy include Scott Ballantyne, Charles Perkins, and Victoria Williams of Alvernia College, who provided information that helped inform the development of the intrapreneurship chapter.

Beyond dedicating this book to Anne (his wife and friend) and Conor and Garrett (his sons), Patrick also wants to thank his sons for putting up with THE BOOK and the time it took Patrick away from them for the several years it was a part of their lives. We also thank David Brightman of Jossey-Bass and the anonymous reviewers of previous versions of the manuscript. If those reviewers read this final work they will see the significant impact they had.

Finally, in 1994 Elizabeth Whitt called her friend, Sandy Estanek, who was the vice president for student affairs at Ursuline College in Cleveland and said her friend, Patrick Love, was moving to the area to accept a teaching position at Kent State University. "Call him, you'll like him," she said. She also called Patrick and told him to contact Sandy. We did get in touch and have been colleagues, friends, and fellow Cleveland Indians fans ever since. We now get to say, "Thanks, Liz" for making that connection. It is an example of "butterfly power" that we discuss in this text.

Patrick G. Love
New York, New York

Sandra Estanek
Buffalo, New York

# 1

# Conceptual Framework

## Lessons from the New Science

This chapter outlines the conceptual framework that informs the remainder of the book. First, we briefly discuss the dominant Newtonian paradigm and the challenge to that worldview presented by the "new science" of the twentieth and twenty-first centuries. Second, we discuss how the insights of the new science have been applied to organizations and how they relate to higher education and student affairs. We develop four concepts from this literature that provide insights to help student affairs professionals think about their work in new ways. These concepts are valuing dualisms, paradigm transcendence, recognizing connectedness, and embracing paradox.

## The Newtonian Paradigm and the "New Science"

A *paradigm*, in the way used here and in the original meaning of the word, is "a civilization's fundamental view of the nature of things" or "the lens through which we see everything" (Schwartz & Ogilvy, 1979, p. 2). A paradigm is a system of assumptions about the nature of reality that is integrated, pervasive, holistic, and internally consistent. A paradigm establishes the ground rules for explaining on the broadest level the nature of the world and the place of human beings. It is the filter through which all human beings interpret the world around them. It is from within a paradigm that human beings understand what is real, what is false, what is possible, and to what they should pay attention. Because one's thinking is so embedded in a paradigm, it is difficult to step outside of it and grasp its outlines. Paradigms are seen most easily when examining other times or other civilizations. One becomes aware of different ways of viewing the world when, for example, one is immersed in cultures of the Eastern world, which see the world in very different ways. Paradigms also become more visible when the paradigm of one's own civilization is changing. The beginning of the twenty-first century is a time of such paradigm change, or what Kuhn (1970) named "paradigm shift."

Paradigms emerge and decline over time. Schwartz and Ogilvy (1979) argue that at any given time there are three paradigms at work—the old, the dominant, and the emerging. Briefly, in terms of Western civilization the old paradigm is that of Aristotle as modified by Thomas Aquinas. The dominant model is the scientific worldview, which emerged from the seventeenth through the nineteenth centuries and which is known as the Newtonian worldview. In the twentieth century, a new postmodern paradigm emerged as scientists discovered aspects of the universe that were inexplicable from a Newtonian view of the nature of the physical world.

In historical terms in Western civilization, for more than a thousand years the world was understood through the teleological lens of Aristotle. This was the dominant paradigm. To understand the world teleologically is to believe all of creation has a purpose and an end that it is naturally moving to fulfill. The purpose of something was inherent in its nature. Aquinas modified this worldview by asserting that the purpose of creation was divinely ordained. The purpose of all creation was to move naturally toward God. Not only were the physical processes of the universe understood in this way, social relations were also understood as teleological and divinely ordained.

Although this old paradigm is still present in religious thinking, beginning in the seventeenth century this worldview was challenged and finally replaced as the dominant worldview by the paradigm of science. Epistemologically, the generation of knowledge within the scientific paradigm was grounded in structured observation, experiments, and facts rather than knowledge based on natural law and authority. Beginning with such thinkers as Galileo, Copernicus, Newton, Descartes, and Bacon, this new epoch became known as the Enlightenment, or the Age of Reason. This new paradigm emerged and nudged off center stage the notion that how things are known is divinely ordained. It had been believed that the sun revolved around the earth because people were told by authorities this was God's plan and because it was confirmed by their own naïve observation. The structured observations of Galileo, Copernicus, and especially Newton changed that. Newtonian science reshaped the basic assumptions about the world, the universe, and humanity's place in the world.

The basic tenets of the Newtonian paradigm are as follows. The universe is stable and regular. It is like a very complex machine. Like a machine, under the same conditions phenomena will behave in the same way. Because the universe is stable and regular it is also predictable. This is the basis for experimentation and the reproducibility of results. If one fully understands and creates the proper conditions then one should be able to predict the results because the results should be the same. The conditions of the observations exist independent of the observer. The purpose of experimentation is to create the conditions under which the same results will be achieved. If that can be done then the result is true. Because results can be predicted they can also be controlled. If one wants to obtain certain results then one should create certain conditions. Stability, predictability, and controllability are hallmarks of a Newtonian worldview.

Scientists and other learned people came to see the world's workings as machinelike. The clock was Newton's metaphor for the real. Wholes could be broken down into parts that would help one understand more fully the whole. Wholes were sums of parts, just as a machine is the sum of its parts. Proponents of science also introduced and preferred the notions of rationality and empiricism. Things were known that could be seen or in some way sensed. This was in contradiction to the previous way of understanding that relied on belief and faith in unseen forces and powers. The Newtonian paradigm is dominant because the underlying beliefs and assumptions about how the world works and humanity's role in it dramatically changed and pervaded virtually all thought, belief, and culture in the Western world. As Zohar (1997) wrote, "Classical physics transmuted the living cosmos of the Greeks and medieval time, a cosmos filled with purpose and intelligence and driven by the love of God for the benefit of humans, into a dead, clockwork machine" (p. 18).

This science-based paradigm has dominated the world for hundreds of years and still has pervasive influence today. However, a new paradigm has been emerging through much of the previous century. Just as the dominant Newtonian paradigm was the result of the emergence of modern science, the dawn of this new paradigm began when the limits of Newtonian science began to be discovered in the early twentieth century. Science itself began to discover that the universe was not stable, predictable, and controllable in the ways it had thought. It is not that the Newtonian paradigm is "wrong;" the old science is "right" about many things. But it is a perspective and, thus, it cannot explain everything. As phenomena were encountered that could not be explained sufficiently from a Newtonian perspective, new ways of thinking were required.

On the largest scale, Einstein discovered that time and space are not discrete and independent. They exist as dimensions in relationship to each other and to the observer. On the smallest, subatomic scale, instead of finding discrete particles and waves, Heisenberg found that they, too, existed as dimensions in relationship to each other and to the observer. Prigogine discovered that complex systems are not stable; they evolve and self-organize in response to constant feedback. Again, structure and environment were not discrete. They existed only in relationship to each other. Each of these observations points to understanding that the universe is not closed, mechanical, and predictable as Newton and his progeny believed. It is open, evolving, connected, and participative.

What emerged in the twentieth century from the work of these and other thinkers has been called the "new science" of quantum physics or quantum mechanics, dissipative structures, and chaos theory. Although the new science was the harbinger of change, it was not the only sector of society that experienced changes indicating an overall paradigm shift (Kuhn, 1970). The notion of modernism with its belief in neutral, objective truth came under stress as well. Postmodernism was a radical response to and departure from the extremes of modernism. Shifts were occurring in the social sciences, management and organizational theory, art, architecture, and so on. In fact, in an analysis of the work being done in the 1970s and even previously in physics, chemistry, brain theory, ecology, evolution, mathematics, philosophy, politics, psychology, linguistics, religion, consciousness, and the arts, Schwartz and Ogilvy (1979) discerned patterns of change across the sectors that represented shifts of a paradigmatic nature occurring at a societal level.

> The point is that things change together. When any aspect of our most basic belief structures is altered, the other elements of that internal framework [that is, the paradigm] must also adjust. We find strong evidence that a number of the underpinnings of our basic beliefs are under challenge. That challenge is coming from a multifaceted revolution of the sort that we have experienced only a few times in the course of our civilization's history: the revolution that began more than a century ago and has gathered momentum ever since involves as great a change as the Copernican revolution or the emergence of the Enlightenment (p. v).

## Applying the Insights of the New Science to Organizations

It is necessary to focus on two principles from this brief discussion as it shifts to organizations in general, higher education, and, finally, student affairs. First, dominant paradigms explain the workings of social structures in society as well as natural phenomena; and second, the dominant paradigm of Western civilization is Newtonian. Taking these two principles together is to recognize that a Newtonian paradigm has informed our views of society as it has the sciences. This is seen more clearly because an alternative paradigm emerged during the twentieth century.

Newtonian science and the associated theories of Darwinian evolution were imported to administrative and management science as models to explain and shape organizational functioning. They are metaphors that shape one's thinking, what one focuses on, what one sees, and what one does in organizations. This framework encourages professionals to view organizations as machines—mechanical, predictable, and hierarchical. They are closed systems that incrementally change, where growth is orderly, disturbances indicate a problem, and where they are in perpetual competition for what are viewed to be scarce resources. Briggs and Peat (1999) argue: "As a social metaphor, Darwin's notion of 'the survival of the fittest' has been used to justify predatory commercial competition and class structure. In fact, the Darwinian idea has become so ingrained that we usually take it for granted that [any organization that fails] must have been in some way flawed while what survives must be 'better.' . . . Scientific ideas that become cultural metaphors are like medicine. They can be beneficial in the right dosage within the right context, but taken in the wrong way, they can be harmful" (pp. 6–7).

Chaos theory and the "new science" are emerging as cultural metaphors helping to see organizations and work in a different light. In the mid-1990s, two organizational consultants, Margaret Wheatley and Danah Zohar, independently began to understand that persistent problems in corporations and other organizations stemmed from the framework from which those problems were understood and engaged.

In the beginning of *Leadership and the New Science*, Wheatley (1999) described her increasing frustration over American organizational life:

> Why do so many organizations seem lifeless? Why do projects take so long, develop ever greater complexity, yet too often fail to achieve any significant results? Why does progress, when it appears, so often come from unexpected places, or as a result of surprises or synchronistic events that our planning had not considered? Why does change itself, that event we're all supposed to be "managing," keep drowning us, relentlessly making us feel less capable and more confused? And why have our expectations for success diminished to the point that often the best we hope for is endurance and patience to survive the frequent disruptive forces in our organizations and lives? (p. 3)

The dominant paradigm for understanding and managing organizations is the view of the world based upon Newtonian science. This is because since the 1950s the principles of science have been imported to the management of organizations. And that science is the seventeenth-century science of Newton, not the "new" science of the twentieth century. Both Wheatley and Danah Zohar (1998) described this Newtonian organization. Wheatley (1999) wrote: "Each of us lives and works in organizations designed from Newtonian images of the universe. We manage by separating things into parts, we believe that influence occurs as a direct result of force exerted from one person to another, we engage in complex planning for a world we keep expecting to be predictable, and we search continuously for better methods of objectively measuring and perceiving the world" (p. 7).

In *Rewiring the Corporate Brain*, Zohar (1997) added: "We live largely in a world of Newtonian organizations. These are organizations that thrive on certainty and predictability. They are hierarchical; power emanates from the top, and control is vital at every level. So, often, is fear. They are heavily bureaucratic and rule bound, and hence inflexible. They stress the single point of view, the one best way forward. They are managed as though the part organizes the whole. Newtonian organizations do not respond well to change. Their primary value is efficiency" (p. 5).

If management is to be "scientific," it should be grounded in science as it is currently understood, not in the outmoded science of the seventeenth century. People in organizations are *not* the same as planets in solar systems or electrons in atoms, and organizations are not machines! One only thinks and thus acts as though they are when one applies the principles of Newtonian science to organizational functioning. The assumptions of Newton have been challenged by the scientific models of quantum mechanics, field theory, dissipative structures, and chaos theory, which assert interconnection over fragmentation, networks over hierarchy, influence over control, and direction over destination.

From these insights, as well as other reading, the four concepts emerged that form the framework of this book. Before addressing those, we provide a picture of where student affairs is today from an organizational and philosophical perspective.

## Newtonian Structures and Student Affairs

The experience of many in student affairs confirms a movement toward governing institutions of higher education from the perspective of business management. A review of recent issues of *Trusteeship*, the magazine of the Association of Governing Boards received by presidents and boards of trustees, reveals a growing interest in bringing traditional business practices to colleges and universities. "Business practices" mean such things as "budget control, cost benefit analysis, hardheadedness, and bottom-line thinking" (Wessell, 1999, p. 29). Bergquist (1992) argued that there are four cultures of the academy: collegial, managerial, developmental, and negotiating. These cultures interact in any college or university to create a distinct mix. It is the experience of many that the managerial culture is increasingly becoming the dominant culture of many institutions.

That managerial culture and the business practices associated with it are grounded in the Newtonian worldview criticized by Wheatley and Zohar. Their critique is thus relevant to higher education in general and student affairs in particular. If one is to be truly scientific in one's approach to management then one should be grounded not in the increasingly outmoded science of Newtonian mechanics but in the emerging science of quantum mechanics. Wheatley and Zohar provide a starting point from which one may argue that to truly embrace "scientific management principles" is to challenge silo thinking and embrace relationship, vision, participation, feedback, and leadership.

But it is not a simple matter of replacing the old with the new. Newtonian science is not "wrong" and has not been "replaced" by the new science. It is not "either-or." A better way to grasp this is to understand that Newtonian science explains some, but not all, phenomena very well. The new science allows for the greater complexity of reality than one perspective could explain. It is "both-and." Schwartz and Ogilvy (1979) understood this when they argued that the old, dominant, and emerging paradigms may coexist. When this situation occurs, as it does now, it is easier to see new possibilities. The same is true for understanding institutions. The structures of the Newtonian institution are not "wrong." One cannot ignore the dynamics in the university that call for adherence to management structures, principles, and procedures imported from business and understood in the traditional sense. These are very real and powerful and they have an impact on how one fulfills one's responsibilities. To be successful one must be proficient in these practices.

Wheatley and Zohar argue that such proficiency is not enough because institutional life is more complex than the managerial culture can grasp. Both new thinking and old management practices are in play. These multiple paradigms are present in institutions of higher education, as well. Although there is evidence that the managerial culture is asserting itself and gaining dominance, there is also conflicting evidence that the university is increasingly postmodern, and nonrational, intuitive, and multiperspectival meaning-making systems are gaining favor.

As discussed previously, learning communities and service learning opportunities challenge the silo structures of many institutions. Kuh, Whitt, and Shedd (1987) in their prophetic monograph, *Student Affairs Work, 2001: A Paradigmatic Odyssey*, laid out cogent arguments about the need for student affairs professionals and the student affairs profession itself to believe and see things differently. Allen and Cherrey (2000) argue that society has entered an era of networked knowledge that will require different mindsets and skills in order to be effective in higher education and student affairs in particular. So we are not the first, but it is clear to us the need to encourage student affairs professionals to think in new and complex ways is still very much in evidence.

Our perspective is this. Once we recognized that both paradigms are present on a university campus we could not simply propose a new agenda for student affairs professionals and expect that this would provide them with any practical tools for creating change within the structures that exist. We recognized that whatever we proposed needed to recombine elements of the Newtonian paradigm and insights from the new science. Although it may sound too pithy, we realized what we proposed needed to be "both-and," not "either-or." It needed to be both the rabbit and the duck. As we already described at the beginning of the chapter, reflecting on the literature cited above we developed four concepts that incorporate this "both-and" thinking. These concepts recognize Newtonian structures and move beyond them. They are valuing dualisms, transcending paradigms, recognizing connectedness, and embracing paradox.

## Valuing Dualisms

Dualistic thinking has been an aspect of Western philosophy, theology, and psychology from the Greeks through the Enlightenment. Dualistic thinking divides something into two opposites and values one aspect of the dualism over the other. It is "either-or" thinking, not "both-and" thinking. An example is the mind-body dualism that characterized Greek philosophy and much of subsequent Western theology and psychology. According to this philosophy, not only does the mind function separately, housed in the body but not interacting with it, but the mind also is superior to the body. The spiritual-intellectual is superior to the physical. Much of Western philosophy, including Newtonian philosophy, incorporates this dualism. Like all frameworks, dualisms help construct a meaningful world but also limit how one views and constructs the world. Dualisms constrain and focus one's attention and perception in particularly dichotomous and often hierarchical ways.

Dualistic thinking focuses on boundaries. In fact, discrete and fixed boundaries are a necessary construct for the creation and persistence of dualisms. If it is X then it cannot be Y. The first step in thinking differently about dualisms is to recognize that the boundaries that exist between elements of a dualism are social constructions. They exist between the elements of a dualism because one believes they are there, much in the same way the boundary between the United States and Canada exists. A view from an airplane shows a landscape that is unbroken. The border is real, to be sure, but it has been created by human beings for specific reasons. Presumably, it could be changed if circumstances warranted.

Dualistic thinking focuses on value judgments and hierarchy. Thinking holistically is difficult. It is often useful to understand something by first understanding what it is not. It is X; it is not Y.

Attempts at understanding focus on what it means to be X. However, dualistic thinking then decides which aspect of the dualism is more valuable. The X is better than Y.

Dualisms are used to understand and construct meaning related to the work of student affairs. These include student affairs or academic affairs, theory or practice, faculty or student affairs professionals, leader or follower, order or chaos, to name a few examples. Assumptions about dualisms, which have been inherited from the Newtonian worldview, shape views of student affairs work and guide practice in the field. These traditional assumptions include

1. One element of the dualism is preferred to the other (for example, practice over theory, order over chaos, leader over follower).

2. The elements of the dualism can exist without the other (for example, practice can exist without theory).

3. The elements are separate entities.

4. Any relationship is one in which the elements' differences and boundaries are highlighted.

5. The elements oppose one another.

A story may serve to illustrate these dualisms. Each year the National Association of Student Personnel Administrators (NASPA) and the American College Personnel Association (ACPA) include sessions on making the transition from being a student affairs professional to becoming a member of the graduate faculty in student affairs preparation programs. Most often the professionals considering this transition have been successful senior student affairs professionals who now are interested in teaching the next generation. However, at one such session a presenter made the point that one of the most difficult aspects of this transition was to recognize when one became a faculty member one left the world of student affairs and entered a new world, even if one had made the transition at the same university. This person argued that it was important to understand that the concerns of the student affairs division were no longer the concerns of the new preparation program faculty member. The new faculty member's former colleagues in student affairs were no longer important. One needed to connect with new faculty colleagues and new faculty concerns in order to be successful as a member of the faculty. The generation of knowledge was now this person's concern. It no longer was effective management of student affairs. This person made this point even though he was teaching student affairs master's students who were graduate assistants and interns in the student affairs division he had once headed and who were being trained to become effective student affairs practitioners. This story illustrates the dualistic thinking characteristic of many institutions. One presumes that one of the reasons the presenter was hired to teach student affairs was because of his successful experience as a student affairs administrator. Yet the structure and psychology of the university separated that previous experience from the person's current role as a faculty member.

By valuing dualisms one recognizes dualisms exist and have meaning. It is not possible to move immediately to overcome dualisms with holistic thinking. The dualisms are built into the context of the institution. To ask professionals to ignore this reality and think differently is to invite frustration and failure. But it is possible to take steps in this direction. The first step is to recognize value in both poles of the dualism. If one is in student affairs then focus on the role of academic affairs and the faculty. If one is a member of the faculty or an academic administrator then focus on the role of student affairs. Do not try to blend them; try instead to see both aspects of this dualism clearly. Ask what each brings to the educational environment. It may even be helpful as an exercise to write these down. The task at this point is to understand and appreciate the value of each pole of the dualism.

To value dualisms does not mean to stop there, however. Once the two poles of the dualism are identified then it is necessary to focus on the space between them. From the new science we know that space is not "empty;" it is a field filled with connection. When one focuses on the two points of the dualism this field is in the background. When it is brought to the foreground one may see new connections and new possibilities. In terms of organizations it is not simply respecting what the "other" does. New thinking presumes a connection is there; that the two aspects of the dualism are not discrete. Each pole of a dualism embodies an aspect of what really is a whole. In the story above it is obvious that the new preparation program faculty member is both a faculty member and a student affairs professional. It is also clear that faculty and the members of the student affairs division are connected by the graduate students who work with both of them. By focusing on the experience of those students it is possible to ask new questions and thus to develop a new relationship despite the silo world in which they all work. Are the experiences of the graduate interns and assistants incorporated into the classroom pedagogy? Do the departments work with the faculty member in placing interns and graduate assistants for the express purpose of providing a more holistic education for the students? Is the faculty member invited to participate in student affairs staff meetings and activities? Does the division utilize the expertise of the preparation faculty in the design of its activities and services?

The traditional opposite of dualism is unity or monism: the two shall be as one. That is not what is argued by valuing dualisms. Instead the two are both two and one. The elements or poles retain their identity, their distinctiveness, but their relationship creates a new entity. Dewey (1980) referred to this relationship as a functional unity. Wheatley (1999) wrote, "In organizations, which is the more important influence on behavior—the system or the individual? The quantum world answered the question for me with a resounding 'Both.' There are no either/ors. There is no need to decide between two things, pretending they are separate. What is critical is the relationship created between two or more elements" (pp. 35–36). The transcendence of an either-or dualism does not result in a new level of predictability or control. When we focus on the individual, the group or system goes out of focus and is imprecise, and vice versa. It results in new understanding and new perspectives.

## Transcending Paradigms

Our intention in the book is to discuss, redefine, and transcend some of the dualisms that limit and constrain the ability to realize the stated goal of a holistic education of students. Consistent with the point made by Wheatley, new relationships are suggested for what has been seen as separate. Again, the point of this is not to make the dualism a unity, but to enhance the view that the elements are in relationship with each other. This is the key to having this book be both forward thinking and practical.

Paradigm transcendence is the next step toward thinking differently. The concept of paradigm transcendence is different from Kuhn's concept of paradigm shift. Rather than a paradigm shift, what has occurred during the last half century is paradigm transcendence. A paradigm shift implies that there is the old way or the new way. There is a change from the old to the new, with the old being discredited and discarded. The two paradigms cannot coexist; they are mutually exclusive. In its own way the concept of paradigm shift is an example of dualistic thinking. To transcend, however, involves rising above, being greater than, and going beyond the limits of something and even incorporating it. When applied to paradigms, transcendence implies that there is the old way *and* the new way. Both exist and both have legitimacy depending on the context. Take, for example, research methods in higher education. Qualitative, naturalistic, and constructivist research methodologies grounded in the new paradigm have gained legitimacy in academe. Yet they have not replaced quantitative, positivistic methods. Each is used depending on the question and focus of the research.

Paradigm transcendence recognizes the existence of multiple paradigms and proposes that one "brackets" each one in order to perceive new connections. To bracket one's experience is a concept borrowed from phenomenology. Once one recognizes that knowledge and experience are socially constructed then one also must realize that "pure" knowledge does not exist outside of one's specific context. For example, one's understanding of the world is framed by one's context as an American of a particular ethnicity and gender in the twenty-first century. However, once this is realized it is possible to transcend this context specifically by focusing on how the context itself frames one's understanding. By putting the social context in the foreground, instead of in the background, one may understand it more clearly. One may recognize both the explanatory power and the limitations of the context of one's perspective.

In paradigm transcendence the "both" and the "and" of both-and are the two paradigms, as opposed to defining the either-or from within the same paradigm. For example, there is the concept of rationality. Rationality is a key concept of the Newtonian paradigm. The first step in thinking differently about this concept is to focus on the dualism. If rationality is one pole of a dualism, what is the other pole? If one perceives dualisms only from within the dominant paradigm the counterpart or opposite of "rational" is "irrational." So the both-and they are attempting to perceive is rational-irrational. Very quickly this becomes an either-or because something cannot be rational and irrational at the same time. But someone who perceives dualisms from across paradigms sees "affective" as the counterpart or opposite of "rational." Both have value and are dimensions of learning. When one begins to focus on what connects the two poles one will discover different possibilities by focusing on rationality-affective than by focusing on rationality-irrationality.

The same dynamic comes into play with other aspects of the paradigms. The opposite of "objective" across paradigms is "multiperspectival" or "constructed." However, within the dominant paradigm, the opposite of "objective" is "subjective." One will notice that the commonality among these within paradigm opposite examples (that is, irrational, subjective) is their perceived negativity. The perceptions of these opposites reinforce the overall perspective of the dominant paradigm.

From the perspective of paradigm transcendence the two aspects of the dualism still exist; however, one is able to perceive both rational-affective and objective-constructed as dimensions of experience. Transcending paradigms helps one see new connections. A different set of assumptions about dualisms and their role in organizations emerges when considered from the perspective of paradigm transcendence. They are

1. One element of the dualism cannot exist without the other.

2. They are not separate from one another.

3. Elements of each exist in the other (consider the concept-metaphor of holography).

4. Their relationship is one of neither attraction nor of repulsion, but one of dance.

5. They exist together in orbit about one another.

6. One cannot understand one without the other.

These changes and shifts in basic views of the world are illustrated in Table 1.1, which presents reconstructed common dualisms across paradigms rather than from within the same Newtonian paradigm. This table can serve as a guide as one begins to understand dualisms from a quantum perspective. The "old" side of the paradigm table describes the assumptions and elements of the paradigm described as Newtonian, industrial, traditional, and Western. The "new" paradigm draws its descriptors from chaos theory, complexity theory, the "new science," quantum theory-mechanics, and Eastern philosophies and cultures.

**Table 1.1. Elements of the Old and New Paradigms**

| Old (Newtonian, Industrial, Traditional) | New (Emergent, Networked, Quantum) |
| --- | --- |
| Objectivity | Social construction |
| Truth (capital T) | Multiple perspectives (truth, little t) |
| Certainty | Uncertainty |
| Reality | Context, perspective |
| Discovering Truth | Discovering effectiveness in context |
| Predictability | Probability, pattern, tendency |
| Determinate | Indeterminate |
| Generalizability | Applicability, transferability |
| Hierarchy | Network, web, heterarchy |
| Authority, control | Influence |
| Mechanical | Holographic |
| Competition | Cooperation |
| Destination | Direction |
| Separation | Relationship |
| Independence | Interdependence |
| Closed system | Open system |
| Disturbance | Fluctuation |
| Disturbance in organization signaling problem | Disturbance as source of new order |
| Growth through order | Growth from disorder |
| Incremental change | Dynamic, morphogenic change |
| Entropy (energy dissipating) | Self-organization (energy infusing) |
| Neutrality | Interaction |
| Simplicity (simple complexity) | Complexity (complex complexity) |
| Linear causality | Nonlinear, mutual causality |
| Fragmentation | Multifunctionality, holism |
| Critical mass | Critical connections |
| Time, experience, change as discrete units | Time, experience, change as continuous |
| Organization as machine | Organization as organism (e.g., human) |

## Recognizing Connectedness

The four elements of the conceptual framework—valuing dualisms, transcending paradigms, recognizing connectedness, and embracing paradox—are related to and overlap with each other. The concept of recognizing connections flows from the concept of paradigm transcendence. The new paradigm encourages a view of life as rife with connections, which can be seen in such concepts as cooperation, relationship, interdependence, network, web, heterarchy, interaction, multifunctionality, holism, critical connections, and organization as organism. Dennard (1996) describes the traditional view of the world as the paradigm of fragmentation, which assumes a disconnectedness among people and between people and their world. Wheatley (1999) goes so far as to describe fragmentation as the problem, which she differentiates from disorder. Chaos theory understands that new order emerges from disorder. Disorder is not the opposite of order; fragmentation is. Wheatley describes fragmentation as the arbitrary and unnatural breaking of relationships. The point is that connections are not optional. The reality is not that individuals are inherently disconnected in organizations but may choose to be connected in some ways. The reality is that individuals are connected in multiple ways but may have organized their work in such a way that these natural connections are broken.

The fragmented view encourages one to see the world as unconnected experiences that require that order be imposed; that the various elements of the world (for example, humans, nature, other life forms) are adversaries needing to be controlled or they will destroy one another. Management theory grounded in the old paradigm emphasizes that control and order need to be imposed by managers if the organization is to be successful. Alternatively, the emergent paradigm encourages one to recognize the connections among people and between people and the natural forces of the planet. All life is in relationship and communication. These are connections that can be nurtured, shaped, and enhanced in order to influence positive change and effectiveness.

Consider the behavior and actions of two hypothetical supervisors. One sees the world as an inherently disordered place in which control needs to be imposed, and the other sees the world as abounding with connections and relationships that shape and influence the behavior of people. How these two individuals might approach the supervisory relationship would be very different. The first supervisor sees each supervisory relationship as a distinct and separate interaction. He or she views the person she or he supervises only in terms of the role that person plays within the organization. Goals and objectives are set, actions and behaviors are observed and measured, and praise and punishment are used to improve performance. The purpose of these activities is to impose control. The latter supervisor recognizes the individual supervisory relationship as occurring with the whole person, and not just the particular role, and within the context of multiple relationships. The supervisor also realizes the individual staff member's interaction with other individual staff members, and the staff itself (that is, the whole) influences the behavior of that individual staff member, as well as anything the supervisor does with the individual. This is also another example of both-and; it is both the influence of the supervisor and the influence of the context and the other relationships.

Consider also the notion of athletic competition. Briggs and Peat (1999) argued, "Athletes love the spirit of competition and become exhilarated when pitted against each other. But we should note that their competition takes place within the context of cooperation. Agreements by individuals to cooperate in teams and follow rules make competition possible" (p. 63). Given a traditional paradigm focus on the importance of competition, our tendency is to miss completely the cooperative aspects of our relationships, a tendency that only further intensifies the competitive aspects, thus in turn further dampening cooperation. The focus in this section is to highlight connectedness and bring it to the foreground.

To Wheatley (1999, p. 11), "relationship is the key determiner of everything." Organizations are webs of relationships. It is through focusing on these connections that communication takes place and information is shared. Wheatley understands information from a quantum perspective. Information is not a "thing" to be shared, or not. It is the dynamic feedback that is always present in any system of relationships. Information is the creative material of organizations. It is through recognizing that information is feedback that new reality is created. In the traditional paradigm, information is perceived as finite and it is something that needs to be hoarded and controlled. Feedback is understood as an optional aspect of organizational life as, for example, when one indicates that one is going to seek someone's feedback. In the new paradigm, information is viewed as a self-renewing resource and feedback is understood as always present. If one is focused on connectedness one will be sensitive to that ever-present feedback.

## Embracing Paradox

The final aspect of the conceptual framework informed by the new science is embracing paradox. Dualisms are about the dynamic relationship of opposites, whereas a paradox is a statement or proposition that is seemingly self-contradictory but in reality expresses a truth. Dualisms or functional unities are closely related to paradoxes. An everyday example of a paradox is that standing is more tiring than walking. A paradox is another way in which dualisms can be transcended even while they remain structurally in place. Opposing elements of a particular dualism are recognized to exist together at the same time. In reference to the paradigms discussed above, the most significant paradox of the new science is that order derives from disorder (or chaos). In the traditional or Newtonian paradigm, disorder is seen as being indicative of a system's deterioration. When one sees conflict as an element of disorder, from a traditional perspective one would be moved to mute or mediate the conflict as quickly as possible in order to preserve the system or organization. From a new science perspective, instead of rigidly trying to maintain a state of equilibrium, that is, the absence of conflict, one instead might more appropriately see conflict as a source of creativity or new growth. This insight is particularly important in considering leadership and the role of politics in the next chapter. As Dennard (1996) indicates, "Chaos can be understood in a nontechnical way as occurring when (1) a system or organism can no longer sustain a particular pattern of behavior in an increasingly turbulent environment and (2) when the system or organism sets about reorganizing itself to accommodate these environmental changes. In this view, conflict is only a symptom of a social system seeking to appropriately reorganize and rebalance itself" (p. 498).

Identifying, creating, and understanding paradoxes is one of the keys to this shift in perspective. Wheatley (1999) asserted that context is everything, that nothing transfers, that nothing is generalizable. This assertion can be used to build a paradox: nothing is generalizable and everything is generalizable. Here is an example: there are approximately 3,600 colleges and universities in the United States. All are surveyed about some issue of importance, such as addressing racial tensions. By some miracle, a 100 percent return rate is achieved. The numbers are run. Do the results obtained tell someone how she or he should proceed on her or his campus? No. Individuals would have to decide how the findings relate to the specific context on their campus. So even the most perfectly designed and implemented social science research is not generalizable. At the other end of the scale, there is a novel about a fictitious college with a fictitious dean of students. This dean is wrestling with racial tensions on her campus. Can this information be generalized to another situation? It can. Again, the context will be important, as Wheatley states.

The way out of this particular paradox is to understand the two poles differently. Nothing is generalizable, but everything is applicable. This is an example of creating or using new and different words or language in order to transcend particular dualisms. Everything can be applied in a particular situation. Why? Because everything is filtered through the experience and sense-making skills of the individuals involved in the particular context of application.

Paradox is one form of dualism that represents the transition to understanding and applying paradigm transcendence. That is the acceptance that two items on one level are contradictory but on another level exist together in a relationship. Examples of paradoxes from the literature on organizations include the following:

- Leaders require credibility, yet effective leaders are constantly having their credibility questioned (Kouzes & Posner, 1995).

- Routine(s) is required for the effective and efficient operation of an organization, yet it is routine(s) that destroys the opportunity for creativity (Kouzes & Posner, 1995).

- "A living system produces itself; it will change in order to preserve that self. Change is prompted only when an organism decides that changing is the only way to maintain itself" (Wheatley, 1999, p. 20).

- The more freedom there is, the more order. "This is, for me, the most illuminating paradox of all. The two forces that we have placed in opposition to one another—freedom and order—turn out to be partners in generating healthy, well ordered systems" (Wheatley, 1999, p. 87).

Paradoxes and dualisms encourage individuals to hold contradictory or apparently contradictory assertions or beliefs in their minds. That kind of mental flexibility is important as one proceeds through the remainder of this book.

Danah Zohar (1998) wrote an article entitled, "What Would a Quantum Organization Look Like?" There is a danger and a fallacy in this question. The fallacy is that there are or could be quantum organizations that would be discernable from nonquantum (Newtonian, industrial, old paradigm) organizations. The point made throughout this volume is that all organizations are both. It depends on how one is looking at them and what one is looking for; one can see a rabbit or a duck. If one is looking for hierarchy, simple complexity, and linear thinking, one can find that in virtually any organization. The same can be said for complexity, chaos, self-organization, and indeterminacy. If one believes organizations are rational and predictable that is what one will see. The rest will simply be noise or static in the system. The goal for readers of this volume is to enhance their ability to see both at the same time. If one works with supervisors who impose hierarchy, pretending that they do not have the power to impose this is organizational suicide. However, that does not mean one is powerless or one must adopt that as one's dominant or sole worldview. One must be aware of it and take others' worldviews into consideration when acting in the organization.

The four concepts presented in this chapter provide a practical method for learning to think differently about the organizations in which one works and to perceive new possibilities within them. To briefly summarize:

> First, one should understand dualisms as connected poles of a hidden whole. Each aspect of a dualism illuminates a quality that is important to the whole itself.
>
> Second, one should focus on the hidden connections between the two poles of the dualism and bring them to the foreground.
>
> Third, once one does this, one should consciously redefine one's perception of the "opposite" aspect of any dualism from a

quantum perspective. Thinking differently means that when one recognizes Newtonian assumptions then one should consciously look for the quantum possibilities.

Finally, living in both worlds will produce paradoxes. Working through paradoxes will also provide new options.

Although it is our hope, desire, and expectation that those individuals and groups who reflect on the issues and ideas contained in this volume and who use them to shape their actions as student affairs professionals will experience greater success and effectiveness in their work, we are not promising or implying that one's work will be any easier. So much of what we discuss in this book is about change, and whether one approaches change from a traditional, industrial perspective or an emergent, new science perspective it will be messy and painful at times. In fact, there are aspects of viewing the world in multiple and complex ways that are "worse" than viewing the world from a singular, traditional viewpoint. When the world is perceived as simple, then the answers to one's questions and what one should do in a particular situation appear to be clear. However, when the world is viewed as complex, possible answers multiply and choosing particular strategies may provoke even more anxiety because the choice may be limited. The good news, if it can be called that, is there can be multiple "right" answers to any particular challenge, and even "wrong" answers when viewed complexly or from different contexts will offer the seeds of "right" answers to try again.

At its most effective, applying the suggestions and experiences in this book to one's own experience may result in a metanoic experience. *Metanoia* is a dramatic reorientation of one's being. In theological and religious circles this type of reorientation might be described as a conversion experience. In one's cognitive development, there is a dramatic reorientation as an individual moves from perceiving the world as inherently knowable and certain to recognizing the world as ultimately unknowable, complex, ever changing, socially constructed, and ambiguous. We argue that such a conversion needs to occur within student affairs as well. Students are coming of age in a world where complexity and ambiguity are taken as givens. Our goal in this book is to provide information, perspective, and challenge to encourage the kind of thinking, reflecting, and experiencing that could result in such a reorientation in student affairs organizations.

# Part I

# Seeing Processes Differently

## How We Work

We begin the content portion of this book with a focus on how student affairs professionals do their work—the processes through which work and outcomes are accomplished. In Chapters Two through Four, we discuss two specific processes about which professionals need to think differently: leadership and assessment.

Chapter Two presents the notion of pervasive leadership, which is defined as individually generated relationships and actions among members throughout an organization focused on struggling together to influence and promote organizational learning and accomplish positive changes to benefit the common good. This process of leadership both emerges from the perspectives of the new science and draws on the evolution of leadership theory and research of the last twenty years. Pervasive means that leadership both should pervade one's professional practice and leadership action should pervade the organization (that is, everyone should look to exert leadership). Pervasive leadership also recognizes and incorporates both political and power dimensions of the leadership process. In addition to defining and elaborating pervasive leadership, the chapter presents ways in which individuals and organizations can enhance pervasive leadership in their own practice and their own organization.

Chapter Three, "Intrapreneurship: Pervasive Leadership in Action," discusses the process of intrapreneurship, which is identified as one way in which individuals can exert pervasive leadership.

Intrapreneurship draws its inspiration from the notion of entrepreneurship and describes a process whereby an individual innovates and brings about change, but from within the institution as opposed to from outside, as would an entrepreneur. It is a form of pervasive leadership because in addition to leadership emerging from throughout the organization, innovation can emerge as well. The chapter describes the processes of intrapreneurship and ends with an extended case study describing a specific intrapreneurial process.

In Chapter Four, "Developing an Assessment Mindset," the process of assessment is addressed. If assessment is ever to become an accepted and integrated aspect of professional student affairs practice, it will require that individuals adopt an assessment mindset and organizations transform their culture to a focus on organizational learning. Developing such a mindset is different from merely assessing practice or outcomes; it is seeing practice and processes through the perspective of assessment. Such a perspective realizes that assessment is about learning and improvement to a much greater degree than it is about accountability and solving organizational problems. The chapter differentiates assessment from evaluation, describes several dualisms related to assessment, addresses both individual and organizational aspects of assessment, and concludes with specific practices for developing an assessment mindset.

# 2

# Pervasive Leadership

Several years ago in a course on administration of student affairs, Patrick asked a group of students to each identify an effective senior administrator in student affairs (for example, director of a function, dean, vice president) whom they knew and with whom they could have a conversation. The students were to speak with those individuals about the role politics and political skill play in their success as leaders. Eleven students spoke with eleven administrators and not one administrator wanted to discuss or admit to the role politics played in his or her success. A few, when pressed, admitted that political skill played a role, but were very uncomfortable discussing specifics. This example represents the deep ambivalence and discomfort student affairs professionals have for the concept and practice of politics. Politics exists and is a reality of organizational life; student affairs leaders just do not want to talk about it.

This anecdote is shared at the beginning of a chapter on leadership because it points to a major undiscussed dualism in student affairs—leadership versus politics. Dualisms closely related to this one are the common good versus self-interest, and reason versus power. As described in the previous chapter, with most dualisms one pole is perceived as positive (leadership, common good, reason) and one is seen as negative (politics, self-interest, and power). The purpose of this chapter is to present a view of leadership that transcends paradigms, values dualisms, recognizes connections, and embraces paradox. So it begins with the dualism of leadership versus politics, exploring, relating, and transcending the concepts, as well as focusing on power and its role in politics and leadership. This is followed by the description and definition of pervasive leadership that emerges from the embrace of the leadership-politics dualism. The concept of pervasive leadership is then elaborated, and the chapter concludes with suggestions for how pervasive leadership may be encouraged in individual and organizational practice.

## Politics

Although a topic of discourse since the ancient Greeks, two classic definitions of politics emerged in the mid-twentieth century. In 1936, Harold Lasswell published *Politics: Who Gets What, When, and How.* The title of this book became a classic definition. Later, David Easton (1965, p. 50) defined politics as "social interactions that are oriented toward the authoritative allocation of values." Like all good definitions, these are deceptively simple. Politics is about deciding, when more than one course of action is possible. As Lasswell put it in his definition, the salient questions in any decision situation are, What will be the decision? Who will decide? How will the decision be made? When will the decision be made and implemented? Easton's definition contains several components that elucidate the complexity and potential for conflict inherent in an understanding of politics. First, politics is a "social interaction;" it is not an individual activity. Individuals may have definite opinions and interests related to any given issue, but at some point they must interact with others. Politics is a community activity. Because of this there is inherent in this interaction the potential for disagreement and conflict as well as agreement at virtually every point.

Politics is not just any social interaction. It is interaction around "the authoritative allocation of values." In other words, the community must come together in some way binding upon all (authoritative) to decide "who gets what." Easton does not use the term *resources*, although the allocation of resources is a political process. He deliberately used the more inclusive term "values." Not only are resources such as money and time allocated authoritatively, abstract social goods such as prestige and recognition also are decided. By "authoritative" Easton does not imply any particular method of decision making. He does not use "authoritative" to mean *authoritarian* versus *democratic* or *hierarchical* versus *collaborative*. He means whatever methods are recognized by the community as legitimate and binding. Inherent in the definition is the recognition that there are many possible methods a community may use to distribute its social values. One person may make the decision for all or the whole group may wait until all have come to consensus before acting. Both situations are equally political. Also, the political issues of decision making, allocating resources or values, determining direction, community activity, and social interaction inform a more complex view of leadership.

Going back to the dualisms, to argue that common good/reason is opposed to self-interest/power is to argue that the right answer to a decision with several possible courses of action could be discerned if reason is used and no influence is required. This assumes a Newtonian view of the world in which objectivity, Truth, certainty, and predictability exist. So, if the right answer is not available, then it can be assumed someone's self-interest will be imposed on the group through the use of some form of power—in the absence of Truth (the answer) there is only my truth! It is, therefore, not surprising that when someone is thought to be acting in only their self-interest, they are perceived as acting politically. The equating self-interest with politics is what gives politics its bad name.

James Madison in *Federalist Number 10* denied there was a dichotomy between common good/reason and self-interest/power. (Note: *The Federalist Papers* were a series of essays written in 1788 to New York City newspapers outlining the rationale for the new constitution that created the United States.) He argued that self-interest always colors reason and informs the common good. "As long as the reason of man continues [to be] fallible, and he is at liberty to exercise it, different opinions will be formed. As long as the connection subsists between his reason and his self-love, his opinions and his passions will have a reciprocal influence on each other" (Madison, Hamilton, & Jay, 1788/1987, pp. 123–124). Madison continued, "It is in vain to say that enlightened statesmen will be able to adjust these clashing interests and render them all subservient to the public good" (Madison, et al., 1788/1987, p. 125). Therefore, reason, power, self-interest, and the common good are inextricably linked together. There is both the common good and self-interest, reason and power: both-and, not either-or.

Madison's argument about the impossibility of separating self-interest and the common good can be illustrated by the following examples related to higher education and student affairs. Many may believe it to be in the best interest of quality education in the United States for some small colleges with limited resources to either consolidate with other institutions or close. What president or board of trustees will do this because it is the best thing (that is, the common good) for "education in America"? To do this there must be a compelling reason that is in the interest of the institution(s) involved. The abstract "right thing" will not suffice. Another example is that some may believe student learning will be enhanced at a given institution not by collaboration between student affairs and academic affairs, but by dismantling the independent structure of the student affairs division and dispersing the functions within academic affairs. The money being paid to the vice president of student affairs could be better used on other things. What student affairs vice president is going to walk into the president's office with that proposal? And if the academic vice president made the proposal who would believe that it was done selflessly? All opinions, regardless of how educated they are or related to the common good, come from a particular perspective, which makes them necessarily limited and partial, and reflective of self-interest. Certainly, student affairs professionals are not immune from seeing situations through the limited lens of self-interest. Woodard, Love, and Komives (2000) cite a series of myths and heresies about the profession as a prelude to challenging the field to reframe thinking and reshape practice. One of these heresies is "student affairs professionals are territorial and self-serving" (p. 13). Based on the discussion thus far, the response would be, "Of course they are! We all are!" The problem comes when people think *we* are not but *they* (for example, faculty, trustees, administration) are. Student affairs professionals need to rid themselves of the myth that when they have an idea they are being reasonable (and not self-interested), but when others disagree with them or choose another course of action those people are being political. Embracing the individual–self-interest, organization–common good dynamic is an aspect of pervasive leadership.

## The Case of Power

Before moving into a definition and discussion of pervasive leadership, it is important to address the issue of power, a concept inherent in definitions of politics. "Who gets what" depends on power. Student affairs professions disdain power as something unsavory. There also is an assumption in the profession that student affairs and student affairs professionals do not have power. This chapter challenges the assumptions that power is bad and student affairs does not have any. Dimensions of power are discussed below in the elaboration of pervasive leadership; however, understanding the role of power in student affairs work is essential to the notion of pervasive leadership. Professionals need to understand and use the power they have, know how to accrue more, and think about that power in new ways. Part of the ambivalence regarding power comes from the image of politics described above. When power is used for something perceived to be right (that is, for the common good), it is good; when it is used for something the individual or group disagrees with, it is bad. When individuals exercise power, they perceive it as good; when someone else does, it is bad. Another aspect of the ambivalence comes from the tendency to equate power with control and coercion. This is not surprising given that one of the classic definitions of power is "the ability of A to get B to do something that B otherwise would not do" (Dahl, 1976, p. 17). In higher education literature, Birnbaum (1988, p. 13) states a similar definition, "the ability to produce intended change in others, to influence them so that they will be more likely to act in accordance with one's own preferences." These definitions perpetuate power's bad name and make it easy to see power only in coercive terms. Although coercion is a form of power, it is not the only form. In fact, Fisher (1984, p. 31) argues that leaders who rely too often on coercion will not be effective in the long run.

## Theoretical History of Leadership

The history of leadership theory serves as a contextual foundation for pervasive leadership. The history summarizes the efforts of the previous one hundred years to capture the essence of leadership, with the goals of identifying, nurturing, or training effective leaders. Several clusters of theories developed and evolved during the twentieth century. The first group of leadership theories were referred to as the great man theories (women were not considered as leaders) because the assumption underlying the research was that leadership and leadership ability was something gained through heredity. This notion actually developed in the mid-nineteenth century in a world society still very much dominated by monarchies. However, even though this approach declined as a serious focus of inquiry in the early part of the twentieth century with the rise of national democracies, the assumptions about genetic predispositions persist today. One need only count the number of times someone is described as a "born leader."

The second group of leadership theories were the trait approaches. It was believed certain individuals had particular characteristics or attributes related to their ability to lead. The underlying belief was that leadership came naturally for some people due to these attributes. One of the goals of this research was to identify the important traits of leadership so potential leaders could be identified and nurtured. Again, although trait theory, as a focus of serious inquiry, diminished by the middle of the twentieth century, the assumption that successful leaders possess certain identifiable characteristics persists and, in part, explains the continuing popularity of biographies and autobiographies of successful leaders, such as Lee Ioccoca, Margaret Thatcher, Chuck Yeager, Colin Powell, and Bill Gates. What the great man and trait approaches have in common is that leadership was viewed as residing in the individual, separate from any consideration of context, environment, situation, organization, or who the followers were. The assumption was that a leader transcended time, place, and context. A leader was a leader and would be a leader, no matter the situation. It was not until after World War II that factors and circumstances beyond the individual leader were seriously considered.

The theories that served as a transition between leadership existing solely in the individual and leadership being a complex interaction between leaders and followers were the behavioral approaches. Rather than who the leader was or what characteristics he or she possessed, the focus in behavioral leadership research was on what the leader did—what behaviors effective leaders exhibited. The goal of this research was to find the best ways to lead. These ways could then be taught to aspiring leaders. This represents a transition between theories viewing leadership as fixed within the individual to those theories seeking to take into account situations and context. One of the behaviors explored under this approach had to do with how leaders balanced their focus on people-related behaviors with task-related behaviors, representing one of the first times followers were considered in research on leadership.

Research and theorizing about leadership increased during the 1960s and 1970s and surged during the 1980s (Rost, 1991). Approaches to leadership study during that time included contingency-situational, influence, reciprocal, and excellence theories. The contingency-situational approaches took into account the need for different behaviors and strategies of leadership depending on the situation, or the expectation that the situation would dictate who would emerge as a leader from a particular group. Influence theory focused on leadership as a social exchange process between leaders and followers, where leaders were seen as attempting to influence follower behavior. Reciprocal theories recognized leadership as a relational process between leaders and followers, and included transformational, transactional, and servant-leadership theories. Finally, Rost (1991) coined the term "excellence theory" to represent the amalgamation of virtually all that had come up to that point. Excellence theory means, "Leadership produces excellent organizations because leaders are great executives who have certain traits that help them choose the correct behaviors so that they do the right thing in key situations by facilitating the work group democratically but forcefully" (pp. 18–19). This definition has aspects of traits, behaviors, situations, reciprocity, and relationship.

The evolution in the study of leadership included expanding the focus of inquiry from the individual leader to include the situation, context, and relationships that the leader experienced. These developments paralleled the emergence of the new paradigm described in the first chapter. Rost referred to the theories promulgated up through the 1980s as being grounded in the industrial (or Newtonian) paradigm. Prior to Burns' work on transformational theory in the late 1970s, all leadership theories had in common a focus on hierarchy, authority, control, competition, separation of the leader from the led, organizations as closed systems, and a focus on change as incremental. Although there was some recognition as early as the late 1970s about the changes occurring in society that averred to changes in the fundamental view of leadership, Rost (1991) indicated the dominant theme in the explosion of leadership writings in the 1980s held to very traditional (that is, industrial) notions and assumptions about leadership, despite rhetoric otherwise. It was, instead, the decade of the 1990s that witnessed the completion of the transition in leadership studies and writings from industrial or traditional views to views of leadership that incorporated notions of networks, webs, cooperation, collaboration, relationship, inter-dependence, open systems, and dynamic change. Pervasive leader-ship incorporates these elements as well as transcending the dualism of leadership versus politics.

## Pervasive Leadership

As Rost (1991) indicated, one of the major failings of the writing about leadership in the twentieth century was a failure to define the term. Authors and researchers articulated what leadership was or was not, but often did not provide a concise definition. This section is structured to present the definition of pervasive leadership and use the elements of the definition as the framework to elaborate upon the definition. Prior to providing the definition of pervasive leadership, four other definitions of leadership are discussed and ana-lyzed to serve as context and points of comparison. These were cho-sen because they represent a sample of definitions proffered throughout the past decade. The four include Rost, who synthesized the leadership research of the twentieth century up through the 1980s, Kouzes and Posner, who translated leadership research into practical implications, Komives, Lucas, and McMahon, who focus their work in student affairs, and Drath whose writing looks to the future of leadership development and leadership studies.

In *Leadership for the Twenty-First Century*, Rost (1991) aggre-gated, analyzed, and synthesized a great deal of the literature related to the study of leadership in the twentieth century. After reviewing and critiquing what he found, he presented his definition of lead-ership: "Leadership is an influence relationship among leaders and followers who intend real changes that reflect their mutual pur-poses" (p. 102). Kouzes and Posner's *The Leadership Challenge* (1995) is one of the most research-based treatments of leadership, as their model is based on the analysis of thousands of personal-best cases of leadership. Their resultant definition of leadership is, "the art of mobilizing others to want to struggle for shared aspirations" (p. 30). Komives, Lucas, and McMahon, in *Exploring Leadership: For College Students Who Want to Make a Difference* (1998), have synthesized much of the recent work in the area of leadership studies and applied it to students and student affairs. Their definition of leadership is, "a relational process of people together attempting to accomplish change or make a difference to benefit the common good" (p. 68). Drath's definition comes from *The Center for Creative Leadership: Handbook of Leadership Development* (1998) and emerges from a discussion of where leadership development is going in the future. Drath defines leadership as a reciprocal relationship among group members who seek to make meaning together in their shared experience.

Our definition of pervasive leadership: **Pervasive leadership is individually generated relationships and actions among members throughout an organization focused on struggling together to influence and promote organizational learning and accomplish positive changes to benefit the common good.**

Each of the four definitions has its merits, but none completely meets the needs for a definition of leadership that reflects the dynamics and lessons of the new science. Rost's and Kouzes and Posner's are from the late 1980s and early 1990s. The concern with Rost's is that it exhibits a continuing dualism between leaders and followers. He does, however, introduce and recognize the importance of relationship in the leadership process. The concern with Kouzes and Posner's definition is that it does not address the leader-follower dynamic. Their focus is on the individual leader, as implied by "mobilizing others." The definitions of Komives, et al. and Drath are problematic in that the role of the individual seems to have disappeared. The focus seems to have swung completely to viewing leadership as only a group phenomenon. The definition of pervasive leadership attempts to retain the dynamic tension between the individual ("individually generated") and the group ("mutual relationships among group members"). Rost was careful to point out in his work that ultimately leadership has as much to do with intentions and efforts as it does with outcomes. This sensibility has been retained in the definition of pervasive leadership ("struggling together to influence"). Rost also clarified that the relationship was one of influence, that is, people and groups influencing one another. Influence relates to the discussion of politics and power at the start of the chapter. The definition also agrees with many current scholars who assert that leadership is about change, and in fact, about positive change, so that aspect of the definition of Komives, et al. is included in the definition of pervasive leadership. The element of organizational learning has been added, because it is a form of change more subtle than is implied in typical organizational change literature. It is the kind of change that addresses the culture of the organization and lays the groundwork for future changes in the organization. The pervasive leadership definition also reflects a world that is complex, chaotic, and uncertain. Leadership needs to incorporate holism, have an emphasis on relationship, thrive on uncertainty and ambiguity, be based on trust, and thrive on bottom-up efforts.

Pervasive leadership implies that everyone in an organization needs to exert leadership; it is not a task left solely to officially designated leaders. In fact, the dualism of leader versus follower, which was so strongly in evidence in the leadership literature of much of the twentieth century, is breaking down. Leadership is recognized as being more widespread through an organization than merely in a series of hierarchically arrayed "leadership" positions. This is not to say that traditional assumptions about leadership and leaders do not continue to hold sway or influence organizations and the people and action within them. They do. Traditional forms of leadership have appropriateness and effectiveness for relatively stable environments with well-defined and well-structured problems (Novelli & Taylor,

1993). However, even in complex and dynamic environments traditional assumptions about leadership are still held by many people, including powerful people who influence institutional life, such as trustees, presidents, and vice presidents. So the concepts *leader* and *follower* will continue to have traditional meaning for many people. In the instance of follower, it may mean being passive, externally directed, and disempowered. For leader, it will mean having formal position power, possessing authority, and directing others.

The notion of leadership must move from the idea of a *leader*, a person, to *leadership*, a competency, that can and should be exhibited by all members of an organization. Leadership must become everyone's business (Astin & Astin, 2000; Kouzes & Posner, 1995). An organization does not need only "leaders," but also individuals who exhibit leadership. Most of the research and writing in student affairs that addresses leadership focuses on organizationally designated leaders. This has inhibited the development of alternative versions and visions of leadership. The difference between leader and leadership is an important, but subtle, distinction. Individuals can exert leadership in a situation, without they themselves or others defining them as leaders. Depending on the situation, different or multiple individuals can exert leadership. To make this point, one can look at one leadership text that provides a "how to" for effective leadership. Kouzes and Posner (1995) base their work on research conducted with thousands of formally designated "leaders." Through their research Kouzes and Posner argue that there are five fundamental practices of exemplary leadership:

- Challenging the process

- Inspiring a shared vision

- Enabling others to act

- Modeling the way

- Encouraging the heart

Any member of an organization, depending on the situation and the culture of the organization, can challenge a process, inspire a shared vision, enable others to act, model the way, and encourage the heart. The cultures of many organizations may punish or discourage such actions (for example, challenging a process) or others may not view a secretary enabling others to act as leadership.

This leader-leadership dynamic is not an either-or situation but a both-and situation. It is not a matter of choosing between leaders *or* pervasive leadership; organizations need both leaders *and* pervasive leadership. Formal leaders are those with authority over budgets, personnel, and organizational priorities. Pervasive leadership does not exist or operate separately from the actions of formal leaders, but ideally engages formal leaders.

## Pervasive Leadership Elaborated

The elements of the definition are used as an outline and format for discussing the notion of pervasive leadership in more depth and for connecting it to other important work being done in this area. The elements of the definition are interrelated, mutually dependent, and mutually shaping, so the information presented in the following subsections is also interrelated and mutually dependent.

### Pervasive: What's in a Word?

The word *pervasive* was chosen because it addresses both the multidirectionality of leadership and its widespread nature in an organization. That is, not only does one seek to influence those "below" in the organization's hierarchy, as in traditional leadership conceptions, but also those considered peers or at a similar level in the organization as well as the formal leaders "above" in the organization. As indicated previously, leadership does and should exist throughout the organization, not just in formally designated leadership positions. Not only do leaders exert leadership, but leadership is exerted by others (ideally everyone) in the organization as well.

Although leadership actions can be exhibited in the smallest of actions and the narrowest of organizational functions, the word pervasive implies that leadership actions also have influence beyond the immediate environment. Therefore, pervasive leadership requires a "big picture" view of the organization and the work of the organization. Pervasive leadership is not just about actions in a particular program or the division of student affairs. It is about academics and the institution, and it is about higher education. This relates to Allen and Cherrey's (2000) notion of systemic thinking, seeing the whole organization as well as the parts, seeing the parts as embedded in the whole, and seeing the present as related to the past and to the future.

Pervasive leadership does not imply that there is no internal structure or no hierarchy to the organization or that there should not be. In fact, there are both formal and informal structures in the organization. For example, Schwartz and Ogilvy (1979) describe the emergent paradigm counterpoint to hierarchy not as anarchy (no structure), but as heterarchy—the recognition of formal and informal, multiple, overlapping hierarchies and structures (for example, zones and circles of influence, matrices, the informal organizational chart). So from a pervasive leadership perspective, rather than no structure, there is complex, pervasive structure.

### Individually Generated: Each Person's Role

It is vital that the role of the individual be maintained in any definition of leadership. This opposes the emphasis being shifted totally to the group or relationships within a group. Leadership does not exist outside of individuals. Even within groups and relationships, it is the individual who generates action and energy. Every individual in an organization is capable of exerting leadership and should be seeking ways to exert leadership. This requires that individuals have a sense of responsibility for and commitment to the success of the organization. For individuals to have a sense of responsibility and commitment they must be able to see the organization from a networked, new paradigm, and big picture perspective.

This does not imply an individualistic or competitive form of leadership. Much research indicates the importance and effectiveness of collaboration and cooperation. This is also not meant to ignore the synergy that often develops from the interactions and relationships in a positive group work situation. The point is that individuals reading any definition of leadership must see themselves immediately visible in that definition. That visibility calls him or her to action.

## Relationships: The Connections Among Individuals

The role of relationships has been implicit in virtually all definitions and conceptions of leadership. Of course, in an old paradigm or industrial perspective the relationship was authoritarian—based on the authority vested in the formal leader. More current conceptions of leadership recognize that even in the most hierarchical and structured organization, the existence of relationships depends on the willingness of both parties to enter into the relationship. Organizational functioning is dependent upon relationships, and the role of relationships has grown more evident in the struggles to understand leadership. Allen and Cherrey (2000) describe connected and integrated networks and webs of relationships that exist in organizations and the leadership relationship. These relationships, of course, consist of those in the immediate work environment, but they also exist and exert influence beyond the program, department, division, and institution. Relationships include those that exist beyond the horizon of one's awareness, that is, people are in relationships with people who have relationships with the people they have relationships with, even if they do not know them and are not aware of them. These types of relationships are implied in the metaphors of webs and networks. Allen and Cherrey (2000) assert that success in leadership is dependent in part on interrelational awareness, that is, being aware of the myriad connections and relationships that exist in and beyond one's organization. This awareness of connectivity is one of the core elements of the framework underlying the arguments in this book.

Recognizing the role of relationships in the practice of leadership also acknowledges the interdependence that exists among individuals and groups in the practice of leadership. Barnard (1938) recognized a long time ago that even in traditional, bureaucratic organizations leaders were dependent on followers agreeing to follow their commands. Leaders would not ask a follower to do something that fell outside of that follower's "zone of indifference." That means there are things followers would not do no matter what the leader said, and there are things they would do if asked (that is, they were indifferent about). This recognition of a mutual dependence reflected a rudimentary form of interdependence that has only grown stronger and more evident in leadership scholarship of the twenty-first century.

## Actions: The Doing of Leadership

For all the focus on vision, values, principles, and relationships, leadership is ultimately about doing, about action. So any definition must address the actions those seeking to exert leadership must take. Of the definitions previously cited, only Drath's (1998) definition does not clearly indicate the need to take action or be active in some way. He speaks instead of meaning-making—an important, but rudimentary, form of action. However, Kouzes and Posner's (1995) findings are almost totally focused on the actions of leadership—challenging the process, inspiring a shared vision, enabling others to act, modeling the way, and encouraging the heart.

Actions to lead begin with the individual. The individual sees the need for leadership, so talks to others, generates relationships, challenges the process, and so forth. These are initiating actions that have to start somewhere. They can only start with an individual (even when a number of individuals start at the same time). These actions form the basis of intrapreneurship described in Chapter Three.

### Organization: Systems of Relationships

An organization is a boundaried formal and informal system of relationships that is an identifiable vehicle for collective decision and action (Argyris & Schön, 1996). Part of pervasive leadership is recognizing that organizational members are connected to every other member of the organization through this system of relationships, and that the organization is connected to other organizations and systems through relationships as well. This is an open system view of an organization, where any boundaries are recognized as convenient and arbitrary social constructions. Again, recognizing connections is one of the basic elements of the conceptual framework underlying this entire book. Effectively exerting pervasive leadership requires recognizing the socially constructed nature of the boundaries that exist in an organization. Allen and Cherrey (2000) describe systemic leadership, where this recognition is paramount. Even when individual action is exerted, these actions reverberate across the web of relationships making up the organization. There are those formally identified leaders who when they "pluck" a strand on the organizational web, everyone feels it. However, any individual action may eventually have powerful consequences. This is an example of the "butterfly effect." This is the notion that a butterfly flapping its wings in Tokyo could set in motion changes that result in a tornado in Texas. This effect was discovered by Edward Lorenz, a meteorologist, who discovered that making even a very slight variation in the data being processed through his weather forecasting models could result in dramatic differences in results. This led to the recognition that in nonlinear, complex systems (that is, our institutions) even small variations, changes, inputs, or ideas can lead to radical change or transformation. Briggs and Peat (1999) explain and apply this notion to organizations.

[Individual action] may be lost in the chaos that sur-
rounds us, or it may join with one of those many [feed-
back] loops that sustain and replenish an open, creative
community. On rare occasions, it may even be taken up
and amplified until it transforms the entire community
into something new. We can't know the immediate outcome. We may never know if or how or when our influence will have an effect. The best we can do is act with
truth, sincerity, and sensitivity, remembering that it is
never one person who brings about change but the feedback of change within the entire system. (pp. 49–50)

This quotation points to the connectedness of the individual to the
organization through the systems of relationships that exist in and
beyond the organization.

### Struggling Together: The Role of Affect and Intention

Pervasive leadership is not solely a cognitive exercise, nor is it solely
a behavioral activity. Struggle represents an affective dimension of
pervasive leadership. Pervasive leadership requires that commitment, courage, and passion be exhibited in the face of resistance,
fear, cynicism, and resignation. Leadership is as much in the struggle and the effort as it is in the results. Tasks of a project in which
there is no struggle probably do not require leadership. Leadership
is not just individual action, it is not just relationships, and it is not
just a group of people working together on a project. There must be
purpose, direction, and focus in the actions of the individuals and
groups. The action need not be "goal-directed," which implies some
ability to clearly define intended outcomes. No, there merely needs
to be intention in the work and actions of those involved. As Rost
(1991, p. 144) describes, "the intention is in the present and is part
of the leadership relationship. The changes, if they take place, are

in the future, defined as any time beyond the present, and are not necessarily part of the leadership relationship."

### Influence: The Role of Power

Pervasive leadership is about influence, and influence is about power. As indicated above, coercion is often associated with power. However, there are many forms and bases of power beyond coercion. These include authority (formal position power), control of rewards, access to agendas, individual alliances, networks, relationships, information, expertise, framing (leverage over meaning and symbols), and personal qualities (Bolman & Deal, 1997). In traditional notions of leadership power emanates primarily from authority, which is the formal power imbued with the position in question. The higher in the organizational hierarchy, the greater the power. One can assign grades because one is a member of the faculty. One can expend college resources and sign contracts on behalf of the institution because of one's position. All student affairs professionals have some measure of this kind of power built into their job descriptions. Different jobs will have more or less authority than another. Budget authority is an example of this. A hall director may have the authority to spend up to $500 without authorization. The vice president may have authority to spend tens of thousands of dollars. The vice president has more position power in this case, but both staff persons have a measure of power that can be used to act. When student affairs professionals express powerlessness they forget this baseline of position power. Control of rewards is often related to authority, given that the type and range of rewards is related to one's position. Student affairs professionals often use reward power when working with students. They use positive incentives to influence student behavior. Authority and control of rewards are ground in the Newtonian paradigm and are important to consider; the rest of the sources of power in the list emanate from the new paradigm and are accessible to all organizational members no matter their status or position.

Like the ability to control rewards, the ability to control agendas of meeting, training, and planning is an aspect of positional authority. However, access to and influence of agendas, that is the ability to have an item addressed at a meeting or being able to add something to a strategic planning process, is less associated with authority than it is with alliances, networks, and relationships. Student affairs professionals often complain that issues important to them do not make it onto the larger institutional agenda. When that does not happen then resources are typically not allotted to address those issues in the ways proposed by student affairs. One suggestion for student affairs professionals is to build a coalition of support for an idea across the institution prior to presenting it, and to work to maintain that support throughout the decision-making process. Once student affairs professionals recognize that one of the major components of power is the ability to persuade others of one's position, they can use different tactics to get on the agenda.

Individual alliances, networks, and relationships are dimensions of power consistent with the notion of recognizing connections. Baldridge (1971) emphasized the importance of building coalitions to influence action in the organization. Getting things done in organizations involves working with others. One is not often able to do something all alone, regardless of one's position power. Bolman and Deal (1997) argue that administrators must attend to "cultivating links with friends and allies" (p. 170). A manager who fails to do so will find it hard to get things done and will lose power in the process. This kind of power requires a collaborative spirit, and collaboration requires mutual influence and mutual shaping of values, intentions, and goals. Student affairs is predisposed as a profession to use this form of power. However, it must be recognized *as* power. If student affairs professionals build a network that includes faculty and through that alliance are able to accomplish something, they have exercised power. The power rested in the alliance they helped form. Again, by recognizing that this is in fact power, student affairs professionals may avoid the myth of powerlessness and use alliances and networks more effectively.

Information and expertise, in addition to relationships and networks, are resources as well as sources of power, and they are addressed in Chapter Five. Information and expertise are extremely important sources of power for student affairs professionals that are often underutilized. Collectively, student affairs professionals are often the campus experts on students. The better they articulate the experience of students cogently to the university or college community the more power they exercise. This does not mean advocating for students (which student affairs professionals should also do), this means having credible information about students and being able to use that information in policy discussions. If one develops the requisite expertise and gathers the appropriate information, one will be better able to persuade others to follow the course one proposes. The more often this happens, the more powerful one will become. This dynamic also works on a personal level. As individuals develop their own expertise in a given area, their power grows. This can be as simple as understanding college processes and knowing whom to call to get things done. Devotees of M*A*S*H know that company clerk Corporal Radar O'Reilly was one of the most powerful people in the unit despite his rank! Most professionals also can remember the feeling of powerlessness that goes along with being new to an institution and not knowing how things work.

Bolman and Deal (1997) describe framing: "Elites and opinion leaders often have substantial ability to define and even impose the meanings and myths that define identity, beliefs, and values" (p. 170). On an institutional level, there is no illusion that this is a form of power typical of student affairs. But it is a different matter when it comes to influencing the culture of the student affairs division or the student culture. Bolman and Deal discuss "symbolic power" and argue that symbolic leaders use symbols to capture attention and to frame experience. Symbolic leaders discover (or uncover) and communicate a vision, and they do this through telling stories. Student affairs professionals do this in many ways. They do this in the admissions material provided to prospective students. They do this in new student orientation programs and in freshman experience classes. They do this through campus traditions. Student affairs professionals try to frame for students what they should expect from their college experience. They maximize certain aspects of experience and try to minimize other less desirable aspects. By doing so they hope to have a positive impact on the students' experience.

Finally, Bolman and Deal (1997) argue that personal qualities affect power. The person who speaks articulately and writes well has a better chance to influence decision making. This is also true of the person who is personable and who has energy and even charisma. This person may have more power than any of the other factors would indicate. Pervasive leadership involves understanding and using all of these forms of power and influence.

## Organizational Learning: Challenging Assumptions

Pervasive leadership is about learning. Without the deep learning that occurs in effective learning organizations, the positive changes resulting from pervasive leadership will be more likely to change actions and activities on the surface. They will be less likely to result in transformative, lasting change. A focus on learning has become much more so the case as society has entered what Allen and Cherrey (2000) describe as a knowledge-based era. They argue that leading in this era requires recognizing

1. Knowledge is infinite, meaning knowledge increases when it is shared, and learning is accelerated through sharing and innovation is increased through collaboration.

2. The increase in the amount of information is accelerating, which presents the challenge to all organizations of transforming data and information into usable knowledge.

3. There are expanding vehicles, portals, and conduits through which information flows into and through an organization.

4. Systemic knowledge (that is, knowledge disseminated through an organization and accessible to organizational members) is more valued and critical, yet current structures work against this.

5. Ongoing learning for both individuals and organizations is crucial.

A major concern of shifting to a knowledge-based view of organizational functioning is that institutions of higher education are organizations claiming to be about the work of learning, yet they themselves rarely exhibit the characteristics of a learning organization. "Learning occurs in them, but the structures, policies, and staff practices do not promote collective efficacy for organizational learning" (Woodard, Love, & Komives, 2000, p. 86). Senge (1990), Vaill (1996), and Heifitz and Laurie (1997) argue that learning and leadership are inseparable. Pervasive leadership is about change. In addition, pervasive leadership focused on organizational learning contributes to the effectiveness of the changes being wrought. Learning results in change and in different actions on the part of the learner, be it an individual, a group, or an organization. True learning (not just the accumulation of information) results in action imperatives. Learning and change are two sides of the same coin.

Learning is the gaining of knowledge, information, comprehension, or skill, the process of creating meaning by coupling prior learning with new learning, and the ability to use what has been learned across contexts. Organizational learning is not just the amalgamation of individual learning, it is a phenomenon of individuals learning as agents of the organization and it is a collective phenomenon (Argyris & Schön, 1996)—people learning together (process), and learning (product) being accessible to organizational members. Organizational learning requires open, meaningful, pervasive communication and access to diverse perspectives to assist in interpreting action in and beyond the organization. Pervasive leadership is both about individual learning and championing the role of everyone in the organization needing to be oriented toward learning—their own, others, the organization's, and students' (Allen & Cherrey, 2000).

## Positive Change: Transforming Meaning

Change itself does not require leadership to occur; change is a constant. In fact, Vaill (1996) describes this as an era of "permanent white water," wherein there are no periods of stasis, no calm stretches to catch one's breath, reflect, and gauge the distance traveled. The reflection and gauging need to occur while remaining afloat and dealing with the forces of change that buffet the organization. Pervasive leadership is about positive change. Rost (1991) used the qualifier "real" for the changes he described as resulting from the leadership relationship. He described real changes as those which are substantive and transformative. Pervasive leadership uses the qualifier "positive" because in addition to substantive and transformative, change must focus on improvement and development in the actions and intentions of pervasive leadership. This type of change is not moving boxes around on an organizational chart, it is not about implementing organizational improvement programs, and it is not about reengineering the organization. These changes, in fact, fall under the purview only of formal leaders. Instead, the changes related to pervasive leadership involve altering and transforming the meanings, values, beliefs, assumptions, and perspectives that people hold and communicate in an organization and that shape their work and action.

When one recognizes the organization as a system, no problem, action, or change can be viewed in isolation (Wheatley, 1999), a given that makes understanding and analyzing such issues a challenging process. However, recognizing an organization as an integrated web of relationships means seeing that intentional change can be generated from anywhere in an organization. Predicting outcomes from actions in a networked world is impossible; however, this does not mean that all change is random and happenstance. Instead, the change that results from pervasive leadership can occur through coordinated communication, nudging, observing, and renudging by many people intentionally influencing action toward a shared goal or vision (Allen & Cherrey, 2000).

The change process is another example of the both-and view of organizations. On the one hand the organization is in a constant and dynamic state of change to the point where Weick (1979) recommended studying organizing (dynamic) not organizations (static). Yet on the other hand, it is the organization that suppresses change as well. Often it is the organizational culture—the shared fabric of beliefs, values, and subconscious assumptions that shape the activity of organizational members—that dampens actions moving too far from what is accepted as the norm of organizational behavior. Pervasive leadership is about persisting in the process of nudging people to surface, examine, and challenge meaning, beliefs, values, and assumptions that no longer serve the organization's best interests, that is, when they no longer encourage individual and organizational movement toward a shared vision or toward the common good.

### Benefit the Common Good: The Root of Vision and Meaning

The phrase *common good* refers to shared purposes and common vision, not necessarily to a majority view (Komives, Lucas, & McMahon, 1998). The words *common* and *community* have the same root, so in exerting pervasive leadership, one needs to be aware of the needs, desires, dreams, aspirations, and ideals of the community or organization. These needs, aspirations, and ideals may not be currently in evidence in the community. Pervasive leadership is about working to bring these more clearly into evidence; to individually and organizationally enact those espoused values and dreams. Pervasive leadership is not about making people happy, since so much of it is about challenging individuals and encouraging them to examine assumptions, rethink meanings, and recognize where they are acting counter to their espoused values and ideals. Often only in retrospect does one appreciate having been challenged to change the way a person thinks, believes, and acts. Pervasive leadership involves calling oneself and others to a life of integrity, authenticity, and congruency.

To benefit the common good, one needs to be aware of the common good. Shared values, vision, and purpose in an organization contribute to the possibility that pervasive leadership efforts will be exerted in such a way as to contribute to the common good. Having a vision and purpose does not dictate particular behaviors and actions in an organization. Instead, it shapes behaviors. The concept from the new science that captures the influence of a shared vision in an organization is the notion of "strange attractors" (Wheatley, 1999). A strange attractor is a concept that emerged from chaos theory; it is an invisible field that shapes behavior. Strange attractors do not control or dictate, they influence. Basically, although action in a chaotic system is unpredictable, there are patterns that emerge. In some cases they are predictable patterns, due to these strange attractors. Just as a snow fence does not allow someone to predict where the snowflakes will accumulate, it does influence the snow in a particular direction and over time the pattern of influence emerges. A shared vision based on core values, principles, and ideals of an organization can serve as a strange attractor to influence and shape the actions and energies of a group desiring to make positive changes in an organization. If organizational members come to some agreement as to core values and principles, there will be a commonality of direction. This will not dictate action, nor will it predict particular outcomes. It will, however, constrain and influence the energies and actions to particular directions.

Pervasive leadership is grounded in both the emergent views of leadership and in the perspectives of the new science. The next section addresses actions to take to put the concept into practice.

# Practicing Pervasive Leadership

The information in the previous section describing pervasive leadership implies some strategies for exerting pervasive leadership and encouraging the development of pervasive leadership. This section provides specific actions individuals and organizations can take to bring this concept to life in their day-to-day activities, including expanding the organizational capacity for pervasive leadership, expanding the opportunities for pervasive leadership, enhancing individual abilities for pervasive leadership, and exhibiting pervasive leadership.

## Expand the Organizational Capacity for Pervasive Leadership

Capacity building is the process of creating the organizational, cultural, and perceptual space for the practice of pervasive leadership. In simple terms, capacity is the size of the gas tank, not how much gas is in the tank. Capacity building is often seen as an important first step in organizational, institutional, or societal development. Capacity building is presented first, but in organizations the capacity for pervasive leadership will only be expanded by individuals who create opportunities and who are willing to exhibit pervasive leadership. This is both-and thinking. The actions to expand organizational capacity for pervasive leadership include examining and transforming the organizational culture, building webs of relationships, creating channels of communication and distributing information, and encouraging systemic vision.

### Examine and Transform the Culture

An organizational culture that supports pervasive leadership allows for risk taking, has the expectation that individuals see the big picture (systemic vision), encourages one to look forward (futures forecasting—the focus of Chapter Eight), expects individuals to take initiative and exert leadership, and encourages organizational-institutional ownership on the part of individuals. There is an ethos of continuous learning, including an expectation of failure, matched with the willingness to learn from failures.

Who expands the capacity and opportunity in an organization for pervasive leadership? The answer to this question represents part of the both-and aspect of pervasive leadership. An either-or mentality would suggest that there are either industrial forms of leadership or postindustrial–new science forms of leadership in an organization. However, all organizations exist with formal leadership in place. These leaders can quash attempts at creating an organization in which pervasive leadership can be practiced. Members of organizations have also been socialized into the situation-specific roles of leader and follower. Professionals need to unlearn negative or industrial socialization regarding leadership. One begins by becoming aware that one has been socialized and enculturated, not just into an organization, but also into particular notions of leadership and appropriate organizational roles. Therefore, the culture of the organization may be the largest obstacle facing individuals wishing to exert pervasive leadership, especially those organizations where the industrial, hierarchical model of leadership holds sway, where an individual leader or a few leaders hold control and power, constrain action, and powerfully influence the overall culture of the organization. The shared beliefs, values, and assumptions of an organization's culture shape structures, policies, practices, and actions. They also shape individual constructions of leadership and the degree to which the actions of pervasive leadership will be rewarded, punished, or ignored in an organization. So the culture can empower individuals to act or it can constrain actions. Astin and Astin (2000) provide the following example of the impact of internalizing the shared beliefs of an organization: "If student affairs professionals believe that they can make a difference in the lives of students, then their interactions with students and faculty and their other daily work activities will reflect that belief. On the other hand, if the institutional culture is characterized by a belief that the work of the student affairs division is not related to the learning enterprise, then the institution will develop academic governance structures and policies that reflect a peripheral role for students affairs professionals" (p. 56).

The point that needs to be made clear is that student affairs professionals and student affairs departments and organizations help create and perpetuate the culture on a campus. They can also help change, dismantle, or transform the culture to one that is more empowering of the individual student affairs professional and one that is more receptive to the actions of pervasive leadership. Certainly, it can be the designated leaders who work to dismantle negative assumptions about leadership. However, Paulo Freire (1970) asserted that it is the marginalized who must become aware of the cultural system and work to dismantle it. In other words, student affairs professionals cannot wait for permission to exhibit pervasive leadership.

*Build Webs of Relationships*

An important aspect of increasing capacity for pervasive leadership is to see the world and work from the principle of connection, rather than separation (Allen & Cherrey, 2000). The difference between the previous strategy of addressing the organization's culture, this one, and the next one (communication and information) is that building relationships, creating communication channels, and providing information are less likely to engender resistance from the greater organization or from the formal leadership (though in some organizations particular types of information are severely controlled). Allen and Cherrey (2000) observe that effective professionals take time to nurture and maintain networks; therefore, it behooves student affairs professionals to prioritize their time in order to build relationships. These need to be genuine and authentic relationships; these relationships should not be built solely on the basis of their instrumentality. Relationships built solely for that purpose are neither genuine nor authentic and will be of no use when through the process of organizational action, the other individuals or groups discover the relationship to be one-sided and they are being used for what they can do or what they provide access to, rather than for who they are.

While encouraging the building of webs of relationships throughout the organization and beyond, another aspect of building relationships is expanding the notion of who is a member of the organization. The full complement of organizational membership is often not recognized by leaving students, graduate assistants, student workers, and clerical staff off organizational charts. An open-systems view of organizations recognizes the arbitrariness of organizational boundaries, goes beyond the traditional boundaries of an organization, and sees other stakeholders (for example, vendors, alumni, parents, community members) as members of the organization as well. This strengthens the web of relationships. *Boundary spanning* is the phrase used to describe extending the web of relationships beyond the boundary of the organization. The argument here is for boundary expansion.

### Create Channels of Communication and Distribute Information

By creating webs of relationships, information will flow; and by creating channels of communication, relationship development is enhanced. So one way to create greater capacity for pervasive leadership and assist with the process of relationship development is to create channels of communication to serve as conduits for information and to link individuals and groups. Simple ideas, depending on the needs of the organization, include newsletters, listserv discussion groups, interactive Web sites, and social opportunities. Given the complexity of organizational life, even in smaller institutions and organizations, it is important to create redundant, overlapping systems of information dissemination and feedback.

### Encourage Systemic Vision

Systemic vision is seeing the big picture. Allen and Cherrey (2000) speak of being able to see the whole system, that is, understanding each other's work, understanding the work of the organization, and seeing how one's work fits into and interacts with other work in the organization and the overall work of the organization. The impact of failing to see work systemically is illustrated through the following story that came through a class Patrick was teaching. The point being made in the class was that the ability to see a bigger picture is not merely a mental exercise, but shapes actions (people would do different things), affords the opportunity to exert leadership in an organization, and thereby helps individuals serve greater numbers of students. Suddenly, a woman burst out "Oh, my goodness! That's me!" She was a part-time returning student who worked as an academic advisor to freshmen and sophomores in one of the academic units on the campus. She explained,

> I just started last year and I jumped right into working with students. I remember thinking to myself in November that I was doing a good job with my students, especially since so many of them were making mistakes related to our general education requirements. I was able to help them correct those mistakes. Helping them made me feel good about myself and the work I was doing. Then in April—after almost an entire school year—I discovered that so many students were making mistakes because the information sheet they picked up at our front desk—not twenty feet from my office—had incorrect information. I realized that I had been so happy and self-satisfied in having assisted so many students. But now having discovered the root cause, I realized that if I had perceived this pattern earlier and corrected the problem, all that time I had spent with them redoing this situation could have been spent on other topics more important to them. I estimate that I wasted more than sixty hours of advising time that year on this issue and I am one of four advisors in that unit. Yet none of us had discovered this. I think it was a student who pointed it out to the desk attendant. Now I know that I need to see beyond my little cubicle; I need to see the bigger picture. I would have served so many more students if I had discovered that problem earlier.

Seeing the bigger picture means perceiving work through multiple contexts and from multiple perspectives. It also means viewing work as connected to action and activity beyond the boundaries of a particular task, office, or department. Encouraging systemic vision in others or bringing this concept into conversations and staff meetings helps build capacity for pervasive leadership.

## Expand the Opportunity for Pervasive Leadership Within Organizations

Opportunity as it is typically perceived is a favorable circumstance that appears in one's environment—an opening. In this case, it is an opening in and through which to exert pervasive leadership. Opportunity is about perception—what is perceived to be a favorable circumstance or an opening is a favorable circumstance. Pervasive leadership is about creating internal images of leadership opportunities; it is about expanding the perception of opportunities. Perhaps serving on a divisional committee is seen as a chore, as an aspect of being a good organizational citizen. But from a pervasive leadership perspective, now it can be seen as an opportunity to build relationships, establish communication channels, gather information, and see systemically. It can be an opportunity to exhibit pervasive leadership. Other examples include conducting community service activities that build relationships between student affairs offices and the surrounding community, performing any divisional or university committee work or volunteer work, and creating connections to other divisions through committees and advisory groups.

## Enhance Individual Abilities for Pervasive Leadership

Much time in student affairs is spent training staff and facilitating their professional development. Given the particular elements of pervasive leadership, training and development in this area can enhance the possibility of individuals exhibiting pervasive leadership in their work.

## Training for Pervasive Leadership

Training topics to enhance individual abilities to exhibit pervasive leadership include systemic visioning, relationship building, team building, group development and the learning cycle, verbal and written communication, and information management. It is often taken for granted that everyone has the basic skills to develop relationships, or to communicate effectively. This is an assumption that needs to be challenged. Another focus can be on helping staff learn how to examine their expectations, beliefs, and assumptions.

## Individual Development and Learning

In many cases, learning to practice pervasive leadership is about unlearning. The following are excerpts from an interview conducted with Rayona Sharpnack (Dahle, 2000), founder and president of the Institute for Women's Leadership and creator of the Women Leading Change and Partners Leading Change programs. Rayona contends that "You are more likely to succeed if you concentrate on transforming your mental framework, rather than on memorizing mechanics" (p. 270), unlearning what one assumes to be true about what one can or cannot accomplish. The following quotation focuses on who a person needs to be, which she refers to as "context."

> Context can be an individual's mindset or the organizational culture. It includes all of the assumptions and norms that are brought to the table. Context is perception, as opposed to facts or data. People don't go off and design their context—they just inherit it. So take anything from racism to sexism to what you think you can and can't do: It's all pretty much inheritance. It's conversations, oral tradition, all that kind of stuff. . . . Most change programs inside of companies don't work because they address content or process, but they never address the context in which both of these elements reside. The source of people's action isn't what they know but how they perceive the world around them. . . .

Only two things can come from practice—failure and success—and they both have to come before any real learning can happen. But we have a love-hate relationship with success and failure—that is, we love success and we hate failure. That's more of an adult phenomenon, by the way. When little kids are first starting to walk and to pick up and drop things, they're fine. There's no judgment associated with those things. Everything's an experiment to them. But by the time people get to be adults, they have almost no tolerance for failure. And that is a very, very dangerous context to have if you want to be a lifelong learner, because the only way to learn is through failure. . . . We want to enable people to lead change, but you can't lead change unless you've got a profound sense of appreciation and respect for learning. (pp. 270–272)

This long quotation addresses a number of issues in this chapter and in this book, but is framed in the context of personal learning and development, including transforming one's mental framework, understanding the role of societal culture and organizational culture and one's socialization into these cultures, the importance of relationships, the importance of risk-taking and failure, and the appreciation for and respect of continual learning. Astin and Astin (2000, p. 55) provide questions student affairs professionals can consider related to the issues of individual mental frameworks and culture:

Are we limited in our abilities as nonfaculty members to affect the culture of the institution?

Is it appropriate for us to initiate new ideas for curricular reform and revision, or do we believe this is solely the purview of faculty and the administration?

How might the choices and decisions we make individually and programmatically differ from our current experience if we believed that anyone could rightfully and effectively initiate change and transformation? How can we fully empower our students, unless we fully empower ourselves?

Is it enough merely to encourage and support leadership development in students, or do we need to model it within the institution in new and creative ways, whether in our role as educators or as participants in governance?

Reflecting on these questions is a good first step in individual development and learning related to pervasive leadership.

## Exhibit Pervasive Leadership

Expanding capacity, increasing opportunity, and enhancing abilities for leadership often are left to those people within the organization who have the authority to shape the organization at the macrolevel. Stopping there would be in direct contradiction to the argument that anyone in an organization can and should exhibit leadership. Exhibiting pervasive leadership does not require traditional followers. It requires fellow travelers; it requires people who are engaged at a similar level and have a commitment to change and improvement; and it requires people who agree to participate in pervasive leadership activities. At times, this participation may look suspiciously like following. It may indeed be following, but the individuals themselves are not just followers; they are both leaders and followers. Individuals who work to expand capacity and opportunity for pervasive leadership and who work to enhance individual abilities related to pervasive leadership are already exhibiting pervasive leadership. One major way to understand pervasive leadership is captured through trimtabbing (discussed under next heading), but prior to concluding with that idea, other suggestions for exhibiting pervasive leadership include

1. Recognizing windows of opportunity created by everyday events to establish relationships, discuss aspirations, discuss directions and common ends, and engage in mutual exploration of values and purposes.

2. Capitalizing on serendipity.

3. Constantly focusing attention on issues of change and improvement by regularly attending key meetings, contributing to agendas, requesting resources, and sending messages about the importance of the work.

4. Influencing policy development at the departmental, divisional, and institutional levels, and beyond!

## Trimtabbing: A Metaphor for Pervasive Leadership

*Trimtabbing* is an intentional attempt to change the status quo. It is a term that comes from shipping and was adopted by Buckminster Fuller as a metaphor for influencing change in large organizations.

Modern ocean freighters are immense vessels hundreds of feet long and weighing thousands of tons. The rudder needed to steer ships of this size is equally enormous, in some cases approaching a hundred feet in height and weighing many tons. Moving such a huge rudder should take enormous energy. But actually, it takes much less power than one might imagine. The ship's designers incorporate the power of the ocean itself to move the rudder while the ship is moving. They do this by building into the main rudder a smaller rudder (a trimtab). When the crew wants to move the larger rudder they simply move the smaller rudder in the opposite direction and use the power of the ocean to move the larger rudder, which in turn steers the ship in the direction they want it to go. They "steer" the main rudder, which in turn steers the ship. The amount of power used by the ship to move the rudder then is actually quite small. It requires knowing how to use the power already available and knowing where to apply pressure to make use of that power. Trimtabbing is an example of new ways of influencing change by involving organic strategies that take into account the nonlinear dynamics of the connected systems and their response to force. Such strategies also require developing an understanding of how the dynamics of a network operate and where key points of leverage are within the system (Allen & Cherrey, 2000). Trimtabbing is a powerful metaphor for individuals or small groups of people seeking to exhibit pervasive leadership and make positive change in organizations, institutions, or society. In the specific case of groups addressing the issue of children's hunger on an international scale, trimtabbing is knowing that a petition with ten thousand names delivered to a Congressperson is less influential than a dozen handwritten letters by individuals. In student affairs, trimtabbing may be volunteering to be on the workgroup of the subcommittee of the committee, knowing that it is the workgroup that writes the policy that is then edited by the larger group. Trimtabbing is recognizing that it is easier to influence policy at the writing stage than at the editing and approving stage. It is important to realize that this is about steering the ship, not turning on a dime. In the case of addressing major issues, the point is to influence direction and emphasis, not reverse course.

---

Everyone can and should be a part of pervasive leadership because it is important for the future of the organization. Pervasive leadership highlights the important link between leadership and learning, emphasizes that leadership in an organization and in student affairs means being a change agent, and that relationships help build leadership as a professional and as a person.

# 3

# Intrapreneurship:

## *Pervasive Leadership in Action*

As described in the first chapter, thinking often is confronted by dualisms. It is either this way or that way that is right; it cannot be both. A person works either within the structure of the organization and adheres to the norms and policies or the individual is creative outside of an organizational structure. Student affairs exists in both worlds: the modern world of mechanics and control and the postmodern world of paradox and possibility. The dynamics in the university that call for adherence to scientific business principles and procedures, understood in the traditional sense—goal setting, strategic planning, budgeting systems—cannot and should not be ignored. However, allowing them to dominate is a dead end. Instead, transcending the dualisms of manager (working inside the organization) versus entrepreneur (working outside the organization), organization versus individual, and incremental change versus qualitative, dynamic change leads to the notion of *intrapreneurship*. An intrapreneur innovates and brings about change, but from within the institution, not from without. It is a form of pervasive leadership because in addition to leadership emerging from throughout the organization, innovation can emerge as well. An entrepreneur starts her or his own business from scratch, such as what Jobs and Wozniak did with Apple. Intrapreneurship takes this entrepreneurial mindset and applies it within the context of an organization. It is an example of pervasive leadership.

The chapter begins with a brief discussion of the dualism from which intrapreneurship emerges. Next, it outlines the steps in an intrapreneurial process, using the literature of business and the new science and making applications to student affairs. The chapter ends with a personal case study of intrapreneurship.

## "The Organization Man" versus "the Entrepreneur"

In 1956, William Whyte wrote a book that became a classic, *The Organization Man*. This book caught the imagination of the popular culture and spawned a movie, *The Man in the Gray Flannel Suit,* and a play, *How to Succeed in Business Without Really Trying*. Whyte's book discussed the new corporate culture grounded in the dominant paradigm that emerged in post–World War II America. His book described the Newtonian organization, the big, multilayered organization whose vision, values, and culture are hierarchical and mechanical in their processes and thinking. The insights and language of science were applied for the first time on a large scale to the processes of business and other aspects of social life. "The first denominator is scientism . . . for it is the promise that with the same techniques that have worked in the physical sciences we can eventually create an exact science of man" (Whyte, 1956, p. 23). "The Organization Man" was the successful manager in that new organization. The language of the book is out-of-date and offensive today (in 1956, Whyte really did mean "men," and "white men" at that), but the analysis of the way the bureaucratic organization works is still relevant.

These organizational men were not bland and colorless, as often believed. They sought careers of spiritual fulfillment as well as economic security. They wanted to do something worthwhile and to make a difference, as well as to succeed personally. But they understood that the best way to do this was through a coordinated effort with others in the group. The problem with this was individuals became less capable of the creative action the organization needed to succeed. Today's Organization Men (and Women) are embedded in the structure and culture of the organization. They get things done through these processes. They know their place in the hierarchy of the organization and work through that hierarchy to accomplish their tasks. Such managers process their new ideas through the same hierarchical structure.

In contrast to "the Organization Man" stands "the Entrepreneur." Business came to understand that the traditional kind of organization was stable but unable to change quickly in order to respond to new challenges or to produce innovations. In the 1950s, the large organization was seen as the model of the future; however, in the 1980s and 1990s hope for the future shifted to the entrepreneur. In the 1950s and 1960s, IBM, with its conformist culture and economy of scale, was touted as a model organization. The achievements of organizations such as IBM, GM, and GE after World War II helped make America the dominant economic power. But by the 1980s that very same IBM and the managerial model on which it was based were seen as symbols of what was wrong with America. The structure that had made these organizations so successful now prevented them from being able to compete effectively. Instead, innovation and creativity came from outside these traditional organizational structures through the entrepreneur. Bill Gates and Steve Jobs were models of this new wave of the future—they operated very much outside traditional organizations. There are many definitions of *entrepreneur*; however, these definitions share a common understanding that the entrepreneur works *outside* the structure of the traditional organization whereas the manager works *inside* that structure.

It is not hard to see why the managerial model is prevalent in student affairs. In large and small institutions, student affairs professionals work in hierarchically organized systems. In this system, it is easier to do the programs and services that have always been done, try to do them better, and reach more students. It is much more difficult to try something new. Budgets tend to get small increases, if any, in an annual process that is locked in. Since very little of what is done is fully discretionary, it is easy to lament that something new cannot be done. It is easier to say, "If only we had the money or the support of the Cabinet or the support of the faculty or whatever, then we could do this." The system, with its management default, makes innovation and creativity difficult to implement. However, in 1985 Gifford Pinchot III coined the word "intrapreneuring" to describe a new model that transcends "the Organization Man" versus "Entrepreneur" dualism. Intrapreneurship is consistent with the insights of the new science and offers a way of thinking about organizations that can bring greater freedom and creativity to the workplace.

## Intrapreneurship

The purpose of intrapreneurship is innovation: a change, development, or enhancement that is a departure from the norm and challenges existing assumptions. Innovation is stifled by the traditional planning cycle based on incremental change and consensus: setting goals, creating plans, taking action, and evaluating outcomes. Instead, innovation is a nonlinear, complex, and creative process. "Innovation is fostered by information gathered from new connections, from insights gained by journeys into other disciplines or places; from active, collegial networks and fluid, open boundaries. Knowledge grows inside relationships, from on-going circles of exchange where information is not just accumulated by individuals, but is willingly shared. Information-rich, ambiguous environments are the source of surprising new births" (Wheatley, 1999, p. 104).

The typical planning process is group-dominated, whereas innovation emerges initially from individuals or small groups of people. Intrapreneurship is a way of dealing with innovation that transcends the group-versus-individual dualism. To be a successful intrapreneur, an individual needs a firm understanding of the organization's mission, which acts like a field directing ideas and activities within an overall framework. Intrapreneurs think and act as individuals but are connected to others in the organization through the mutual understanding of the mission. An intrapreneur acts for the common good. Acting for the common good, as defined in the pervasive leadership chapter, does not require consensus or even majority opinion to proceed.

Intrapreneurship is grounded in both the dominant and emergent paradigms; that is, it is an example of paradigm transcendence. Although there are step-by-step, mechanical steps to the process, focusing solely on those miss the point, highlight only the dominant paradigm aspects of the process, and miss the insights gained by the emergent paradigm. Pinchot (1985) included typical planning steps such as coming up with the innovative idea, gathering feedback, creating a core group of supporters, developing a plan for implementation, gathering resources, and implementing the plan. These *are* all part of the intrapreneurship process; however, the process is more than that as well. Added to these aspects are paying attention to ideas (and recognizing their source), pursuing ideas in the face of obstacles, being aware of naturally occurring feedback, carefully soliciting specific feedback, recruiting a core group, and utilizing organizational slack.

## Pay Attention to Ideas

Everyone has had the experience of coming up with an idea that did not arise from a review of the literature, a formal needs assessment, or a strategic planning process. Ideas that appear to come from nowhere often fade away with little more than fleeting attention. This should not happen, because these intuitions are the foundation of innovation. Although not all ideas are good ideas and not all ideas should be implemented, our point is that many good ideas get discarded before they even have the opportunity to be critically considered.

Recognizing connectedness, as argued in Chapter One, encourages individuals to realize that such ideas arise within the context of relationships and with the influence of the group. Even when acting and thinking as individuals, people are not insulated from the influence of the group in organizational settings. The mission of the institution, experience gained, everyday observations, and interactions with others over time all create the "field" for innovation. In short, inspirations that appear to come from out of the blue do not come from out of the blue. They are part of that pattern of invisible connections among organizational members. Realizing this should encourage professionals to pay attention to ideas that pop into their heads. Because of the invisible web of connections, a seemingly unrelated comment in a meeting or something casually observed can trigger an idea at a later point in time. Carefully listening to these ideas is important because most professionals live and work in environments that suppress or teach them to ignore their internal voices. The beginning of the intrapreneurial process is when one idea "sticks" and becomes an inspiration—an idea that generates passion and enthusiasm within the individual.

### Pursue Ideas in the Face of Obstacles

Intrapreneurship is about possibilities, and possibilities live in the future. Obstacles to change and innovation typically are rooted in the past. The inclination with seemingly "out of bounds" ideas is to immediately think of all the barriers and all the reasons that the idea will not work. Some ideas appear to fade away, but most are actively dismissed as unreasonable, undoable, unsupportable, or impossible. Every institution has barriers that exist within its structure, policies, traditions, cultures, and people. However, as described in the next chapter on developing an assessment mindset, the more formidable barriers are those that exist within the individual—the assumptions about what is right, proper, and possible in a given context. We *think* these are organizational obstacles, but they are not, they exist within us, not out there! Organizational obstacles do exist, but they only arise when the idea is articulated in some manner to organizational members or units. Until that moment the only obstacles in play are internal—fear, lack of confidence, doubt, pride, and so forth.

Pursuing ideas in the face of organizational obstacles highlights the individual-group dualism aspect of the intrapreneurial process. Although the role of relationships and interconnectedness is vital, the role of the individual must be maintained as well. In fact, intrapreneurship presents a significant cultural challenge to student affairs professionals because it begins as an individualistic concept, where the individual pursues an idea in the face of organizational resistance. Student affairs professionals operate in a culture that is about community, collaboration, cooperation, teamwork, and partnerships—all of which are eventually brought into the intrapreneurial process—and where the role of the individual is often diminished, denigrated, or overlooked. Therefore, one must make a conscious and persistent effort to presume that the inspiring idea can work. One encouragement to keep ideas alive long enough to play with them and critically analyze them is to consider the "butterfly effect" mentioned in the first chapter. Of course, no one can predict which idea or comment will set in motion the process that leads to dramatic change, but it should provide professionals with a healthy respect for any idea.

### Be Aware of Naturally Occurring Feedback

Most organizations collect structured feedback as part of assessment processes, and make decisions based upon the feedback. But from a new paradigm perspective, the environment is providing feedback all the time. A popular management book in the 1980s, *The One Minute Manager* (Blanchard & Johnson, 1982), incorporated this insight. A good manager did not sit in his or her office or in meetings all day. She or he walked around, observed what was happening, and talked to people. In this way the manager received more useful feedback than from just reading reports prepared in advance. Feedback on an idea can be provided by people met along the way and from observations. The nonverbal feedback present in the environment can be observed. A colleague who was the vice president for student affairs at a large institution said she took a walk around campus every afternoon. Not only did it provide her with some needed exercise but she felt she had a much more complete picture of what was going on around campus. Her staff was always surprised at how in touch she was.

### Carefully Solicit Specific Feedback

At first, the idea should be shared with a few trusted friends and colleagues. The idea should only be shared with one's supervisor if that person is considered a trusted colleague. In management structures ideas are often taken immediately to one's supervisor. It is possible that the supervisor will represent an organizational obstacle by explaining why this idea cannot be implemented at this time, or ask for all the appropriate research and documentation, or put the idea into the appropriate planning channels right away. This is the way most managers have been trained to think. Traditional management practice often inhibits innovation rather than promotes it. Of course, one's supervisor is brought in at some point but it is usually later in the process. Again, this depends on one's supervisor and one's relationship with that supervisor. After obtaining initial feedback from trusted colleagues and friends, feedback on the idea should be collected from other diverse sources across institutional boundaries. Anyone who might be a potential user of the new idea or anyone who would be important to the implementation of the idea should be considered. Use the concept of "snowball sampling," in which people are asked, "Who else should I talk to?" or "Who might have a different perspective on this?" This is a way to gain a diversity of feedback. Feedback shapes and refines the idea, and at the same time sells the idea to others. A willingness to involve others in the development of a plan creates support essential to successful implementation. Feedback may also make clear to the potential intrapreneur that the idea is not workable or may actually run counter to the common good. That is a positive outcome as well.

## Recruit a Core Group

One person alone can implement very few ideas. This is true even when the initial inspiration comes from one person. As feedback is solicited from friends and colleagues, other people need to be recruited to join in this venture. These persons need similar enthusiasm for the idea and they should contribute to refining it. The various talents, constituencies, and perspectives the project will need to succeed should be incorporated as the core group is recruited.

## Utilize Organizational Slack

All new ventures require resources. Resources are vital to organizational functioning, so much so that the next section of the book (Part II) is dedicated to thinking about them in new and different ways. Resources go beyond money, and include time, staff, people, space, equipment, supplies, physical plant, information, relationships, expertise, and experience. The people recruited for the core group are resources that contribute to the possible success of the idea. Typically, professionals believe that ideas do not get beyond the dreaming phase because there is no money in the budget to support them. This is an internal obstacle and ignores that there may be other resources to support the activity. Also, money is but one resource, because even if there is money, but core group members have no time to invest in the idea, the project will not be implemented.

Organizational slack describes the excess resources that exist in an organization in the form of underutilized or extra personnel, spare time, unused capital, extra supplies, and so forth. Too much or too little slack results in competitive disadvantages, organizational stress, and reduced performance (Cyert & March, 1963). The intrapreneur needs to find forms of organizational slack that can be applied to the implementation of the innovation. Pinchot (1985), in recognizing the need for resources, argued that projects need to find "intracapital," that is, internally generated resources that act like venture capital to support creative start-up projects. If the organization does not have formal intracapital available, one can get a project off the ground by "bootlegging" the money, time, and talent one needs by looking for organizational slack. Such bootlegging activities can include meeting away from work or after hours to discuss the blossoming ideas and taking money from accounts under one's control and pooling these funds to get the idea started. All of these are ways for ideas to emerge even in the most rigid system if the people involved are committed to them. Additional ways of thinking about resources and utilizing organizational slack are addressed in the next section.

Intrapreneurship provides a way that values the dualism of incorporating some of the insights of the new science while recognizing that most of student affairs professionals work in hierarchical organizations grounded in the old science. Intrapreneurship challenges student affairs professionals not to get bogged down in the everyday managerial tasks of work, but to stay in touch with the mission, one's students, and one's self. It challenges professionals to be attuned to the constant ideas one has and the feedback one is receiving, and be ready to respond. There are also lessons for those who supervise staff. Since most professionals work in hierarchical organizations, those who supervise are in a position to create environments to promote an intrapreneurial mindset within staff members. This can include creating intracapital (both by setting aside money and recognizing and using organizational slack for innovative ideas), encouraging staff to generate ideas they are passionate about, being a sponsor of innovation, encouraging cross-institutional activities, and intentionally bringing people together from different parts of the institution.

Each of the chapters of this book has sections with some practical steps to use in practice. As we discussed the idea of intrapreneurship and its connection to pervasive leadership, we realized that Sandy recently had been involved in such an intrapreneurial venture, and that her thoughts and experience represent how it is possible to rationalize (that is, make rational, predictable) even the most creative and nonlinear of processes. The project was the Institute for Student Affairs at Catholic Colleges. This final section is written in the first person by Sandy, reflecting on this experience.

## Intrapreneurship and Pervasive Leadership in Action: The Institute for Student Affairs at Catholic Colleges

The Institute for Student Affairs at Catholic Colleges (ISACC) was a five-day summer program for student affairs professionals who work at Catholic colleges and universities. The program was held each summer in late July from 1996 through 1999 on the campus of John Carroll University in the suburbs of Cleveland, Ohio. More than 220 student affairs professionals from fifty-nine Catholic institutions across the United States, Canada, and Lebanon attended ISACC during its four years. The program was sponsored by the Association of Catholic Colleges and Universities (ACCU) and funded in part by the Lilly Endowment. ISACC was my idea initially, and I served as its director for all four years. By 1999, others were equally involved in the leadership of the institute. We decided that instead of continuing ISACC in its current form, we would move to create a permanent organization of student affairs professionals working at Catholic institutions that would meet annually. The Association of Student Affairs at Catholic Colleges and Universities (ASACCU) was founded in 1999 and continues today. In this way the ISACC project has had a significant impact on Catholic higher education. ISACC is an example of butterfly power. There was no thought at the beginning that the project would have the impact and longevity it has had.

ISACC was also my dissertation project. My doctoral program at the Union Institute and University allowed for a nontraditional Project Demonstrating Excellence (PDE) as an alternative to a traditional dissertation. One such alternative is a "social action project and contextual essay." In other words, the program allowed someone to do something to address a problem and analyze it for a PDE. This is what I did. I planned the pilot project for ISACC and described the process in two chapters. I grounded the project in the literature base and discussed it in two other chapters. And I evaluated the program by using an instrument that I developed and described the results in another chapter.

When I wrote the chapter describing the process of ISACC's creation I wrote that the "process of development was grounded in the discussions of program development contained in student development literature" (Estanek, 1997, p. 40). I cited Barr and Keating (1985) and Komives and Woodard (1996) and I wrote that I followed the planning process outlined by Moore and Delworth (1976) in *A Training Manual for Student Service Program Development*. I wrote the following:

> The model they proposed consisted of five steps: (1) initiation of the program, (2) the planning process, (3) the pilot project, (4) full implementation, and (5) refinement. Initiation of the program included conducting a needs assessment, developing an idea for a program that responds to the need, assembling those who will conduct the program, and developing the necessary resources. The planning process included agreeing upon appropriate goals and developing the structure that will accomplish the goals of the program. The next step was to develop a pilot project and to conduct formative evaluation. What was learned then was incorporated into the program which was launched on a full-scale level and refined even more. The development of the ISACC Institute followed this process. (Estanek, 1997, pp. 41–42)

This description is not untrue per se, but it does not tell the whole story of the creation of ISACC. In fact, I did not follow the steps as outlined in the training manual always in the order in which they are presented. For example, I did not have the goals of the project worked out in advance of developing the program to implement them. The goals emerged as we developed the institute. I did not have the idea of ISACC and then assemble those who would assist in the program's implementation. Many people participated in the dialogues that created the institute. What I did in my dissertation was to distill moments from the creative process after the fact, and fit them retroactively into the rational, old paradigm model presented in the literature.

I did this because it was expected. This is a good example of the Newtonian model forcing me to ignore the chaotic process of creation as it really was. I made it sound like I had the whole thing planned out before I started. I did not. I made it sound like I created it alone. I did not. We did develop goals, we did seek and receive support and funding, and we did solicit and use specific feedback, but the process in reality looked more like what is described in this chapter than it did in my own dissertation. To end this chapter, then, I briefly retell the story of the beginning of the Institute for Student Affairs at Catholic Colleges, putting back all the chaotic elements and creative energy.

In my dissertation I wrote that the idea for the institute grew out of a research project I conducted in 1994 (Estanek, 1997). Again, this is true but I left out the chaotic, creative moments that had occurred previously. Had those initial experiences not occurred, the research project itself would not have been conducted. In 1994 I was serving as the vice president for student services at a Catholic women's college. I received a sample brochure on women's health issues from the American College Health Association. The brochure had good information in it, but it also had a small section on birth control I knew might be problematic for a Catholic college. I shared the brochure at a Cabinet meeting before purchasing it. There was a lengthy discussion and in the end I was not permitted to use the brochure.

I was frustrated because there was much that was very good in the brochure. I wrote to the Association of Catholic Colleges and

Universities and argued that "somebody should" develop materials for use at Catholic institutions, since we could not use the materials coming to us from the mainstream culture. I thought from my managerial and bureaucratic perspective that the people at ACCU were the people I should contact to do something. From Pinchot's (1985) perspective, I immediately thought to take my concern to a superior, in this case my national association, to solve the problem I had identified. I was not yet an intrapreneur because it never dawned on me that I could do something myself. I figured my letter would be the end of it, but the following fall I received a letter from the executive director inviting me to a meeting about planning a national symposium on Catholic higher education to be held in 1995.

I went to that meeting in Washington, D.C., and during the discussion it was clear there was very little known about student affairs at Catholic institutions. I complained that initial plans for the symposium did not include programs on student affairs, and I lobbied for such a session to be included. Someone on the committee suggested that perhaps I would be willing to do a study and present my findings at the symposium. I was working on my doctorate at the time and thought I could use the research practice so I agreed.

That is the research project I referred to in my dissertation, but I still did not have the idea for ISACC. The idea came through the research project itself and the conversations that ensued because of it. Using a list provided by ACCU, I surveyed the senior student affairs officers at Catholic colleges and universities in the United States. I discovered through the survey that many of my colleagues shared the problems I faced on campus and shared my frustrations. It was clear from my research that our presidents and our staffs expected us to be knowledgeable about both student development and the Catholic tradition, and be able to integrate these perspectives and apply them to issues on campus. It was also clear that the senior student affairs officers understood and supported this expectation but did not know how to fulfill it. Most believed they did not have a sufficient understanding of the Catholic tradition and there was no place to learn and no one to talk to about the issues they faced.

Based upon this research, which was both quantitative and qualitative, the idea of the institute began to percolate, and I slowly moved from "somebody should" to "maybe I could." Frankly, I do not remember when the idea that I could create such a place as my doctoral PDE came to me, but I do remember the first thing I did was call a friend of mine who also worked in Catholic higher education to ask him what he thought of the idea. We agreed to talk about it over dinner. What I do remember is that the initial plans for ISACC were drawn on paper tablecloths at an Italian restaurant in Arlington, Virginia!

In retrospect I realized that I collected informal and formal feedback, and the idea itself was formed in these conversations. I was also "pre-selling" the idea (Pinchot, 1985). I talked to my doctoral committee, and they supported the project for my PDE. I talked to people around the country and asked several whether they would be interested in joining the project if it got off the ground. Over time, a core group emerged. I finally talked to my president to solicit institutional support for the project, to which she agreed. Again in retrospect, I find myself giving order and clarity to a process that was open, fluid, and full of serendipity. One of the lessons of intrapreneurship is that the process should be very open at the beginning and only gradually should structure be added. But ultimately structure and institutional support are needed. Even then, however, one should be prepared for the unexpected and be sensitive to continuing feedback.

I gave the presentation on my research at the ACCU symposium in August 1995. I invited some of my colleagues to join me on a panel as part of the presentation. We decided to bring up the idea of the institute to see what support there was for the idea. We gave our program twice and at each session people thought it was a good idea and thought they would attend. What we did not know at the time was that attending one of the sessions was a program officer from the Lilly Endowment. She became a sponsor, in Pinchot's (1985) sense of the word, as did the staff of ACCU and my own president. As a result, we received a Lilly Endowment grant in February 1996 and ISACC became a reality that following July.

ISACC made a difference in Catholic higher education and in the lives of many of the participants. It has received many kudos. It is an example of "quantum thinking" in which the result is greater than the sum of its parts. Briggs and Peat tell us that "this first lesson of chaos is that creativity is available to everyone" (1999, p. 28). Intrapreneurship as a form of pervasive leadership is also available to everyone.

# 4

# Developing an Assessment Mindset

The concluding chapter in Part One on rethinking processes focuses on the process of assessment. The topic of assessment has been growing and proliferating in student affairs for more than a decade. Ever since the Student Learning Imperative (American College Personnel Association [ACPA], 1994) forcefully challenged student affairs professionals to put student learning at the center of student affairs work, the topic of assessment—especially the assessment of student learning outcomes—has edged its way into student affairs discourse (Love & Yousey, 2001) and student affairs practice. This increased focus is especially the case in national student affairs organizations, which have sponsored conferences and workshops on the topic. NASPA's *NetResults* E-zine has a regular column on assessment practice in student affairs. Also, very popular books have been published on assessment practice in student affairs (Schuh & Upcraft, 2001; Upcraft & Schuh, 1996). Yet for all the action and rhetoric, the struggle continues for most student affairs professionals and programs to move beyond discourse and beyond individual assessment projects or programs focused on particular problems to integrating and incorporating assessment as a fundamental aspect of effective student affairs practice.

Assessment is about learning—personal and organizational learning—and it is about improvement. Individual reflective practice involves aspects of assessment and so do efforts at organizational and administrative improvement. Some of the struggle to incorporate assessment into individual and organizational practice is due in part to the fact that many beliefs about and practices related to it are grounded in old paradigm assumptions and to the failure to recognize the importance of assessment in individual, as well as in organizational, practice. Instead, assessment is too often seen as something being imposed from outside or from above, something at best tangential to student affairs work, which implies that to excise assessment practice would result in no overall loss for the organization.

The chapter begins with defining assessment and differentiating it from evaluation. Also described are three dualisms related to assessment whose poles influence the practice of assessment: (1) assessment for accountability and assessment for improvement, (2) problem-generated assessment and development-directed assessment, and (3) assessment of student learning outcomes and assessment of administrative practice. This is followed by sections on individual and organizational aspects of assessment: developing an assessment mindset and creating learning organizations. The chapter concludes with information and suggestions on how to begin incorporating assessment in a student affairs organization.

Individual and organizational aspects of professional practice are intertwined and interconnected. If organizations are to improve, change, and grow, individuals need to change and grow as well. If student learning outcomes are to be assessed and improved, individual practice needs to be assessed and improved as well. This goes the other way as well. If enough individuals are focused on growing and improving, in most cases, organizations will follow suit. Probably not in a predictable fashion, but, as is the case in chaotic systems, individual change and action has the potential of causing larger, more widespread changes in the greater system or organization.

## Assessment Defined

The definition of assessment used in this chapter is based on, but differs from the definitions of Schuh and Upcraft (2001). Our definition is: **On-going efforts to gather, analyze, and interpret evidence which describes individual, programmatic, or institutional effectiveness and using that evidence to improve practice.**

Assessment and evaluation are often used synonymously, because there are overlapping aspects of their definitions. Until recently, evaluation was the dominant focus in administrative and organizational practice. During the last couple of decades, assessment has grown to be the prevailing term both because of its focus, as described below, but also because of the negative connotation of the word *evaluation*. Many people and organizations have experienced evaluation processes as punishment and as painful, non-developmental experiences, especially individual performance appraisals. The terms *assessment* and *evaluation* were further confused because, as more attention began to be paid to assessment, some evaluation practices were relabeled assessment probably to "jump on the bandwagon" of assessment and to avoid the negative connotation of evaluation. In some instances, relabeling led to suspicion about both terms.

Upcraft and Schuh (1996, Schuh & Upcraft, 2001) have forcefully moved assessment toward the center of student affairs discourse and practice. The definition in this chapter, however, diverges from their definitions of assessment and evaluation, as they have specifically stated them. They define assessment as "any effort to gather, analyze, and interpret evidence which describes institutional, departmental, divisional, or agency effectiveness" (1996, p. 18). (Note: They specifically indicate that they are not focusing their work on individual dimensions of assessment, as will be the case in this chapter.) They then define evaluation as "any effort to use assessment evidence to improve institutional, department, division, or agency effectiveness" (1996, p. 19). According to these definitions, assessment describes effectiveness and gathers data; evaluation uses these descriptions and data to improve effectiveness. So according to their definition, assessment does not imply or require action beyond collecting and understanding data. All the action is left to activities they defined as evaluation. Although technically and traditionally what they defined as assessment is a form of assessment, it does not capture how assessment is defined in action in higher education and student affairs today. Schuh and Upcraft try too hard to separate the two terms, rather than differentiating what are really two overlapping concepts. This overlap in definition is a reason that the two terms are so often used synonymously. Schuh and Upcraft's definitions were combined, the focus was shifted from discrete practice to continuous practice, and the individual dimension was added to arrive at the definition of assessment used in this chapter.

The definition for evaluation draws both on the work of Schuh and Upcraft and that of Worthen, Sanders, and Fitzpatrick (1997). It is: **Evaluation consists of efforts to gather, analyze, and interpret evidence to determine an evaluation focus (for example, student learning, administrative practice), quality, utility, effectiveness, or significance in relation to stated criteria or other standards and, in cases where the object falls short, use that evidence to help the evaluation object reach an adequate level of performance.**

According to these definitions, assessment asks, How effective is this practice? and How can it become more effective? Evaluation asks, Is this practice effective enough? If not, how can it become effective enough? Evaluation renders judgment. Both seek to improve outcomes, though in many cases evaluation stops with rendering a judgment. According to the definitions cited above, collecting information on a program or the performance of an employee to help with improvement is assessment. Receiving a grade for a course or conducting a year-end performance review to determine raises are examples of evaluation. Finally, although Schuh and Upcraft (2001) significantly differentiate assessment and evaluation in their definitions, they then collapse them and focus on and title their work *Assessment Practice in Student Affairs*, not *Assessment and Evaluation Practice in Student Affairs*.

## Recognizing Dualisms in Assessment

There are at least three dualisms in assessment practice that need to be distinguished in any discussion of the topic because the elements of each differentially influence the focus and practice of assessment. As stated at the beginning of the chapter, these dualisms are (1) assessment for accountability and assessment for improvement, (2) problem-generated assessment and development-directed assessment, and (3) assessment focusing on student learning outcomes and assessment focused on administrative practice.

### Assessment for Accountability and Assessment for Improvement

The poles of this dualism are two basic reasons that individuals or groups assess practice. Assessment for accountability is to prove worth. This can be to prove to ourselves that one is an effective professional. It can be to provide evidence to supervisors or senior student affairs officers (SSAOs) that the investment of resources in a program area or department is worthwhile. Institutionally, it is about demonstrating to accrediting agencies that the institution is worthy of endorsement. Such a focus of assessment is grounded in old paradigm assumptions, including the belief that one can precisely measure worth and effectiveness of practice, and that practice is linearly related to outcomes. Assessment for accountability is important to practice and in many cases it is unavoidable, because it is this issue that is driving the external pressure to conduct assessment (Scott, 1996; Upcraft & Schuh, 1996). Also, this aspect of the dualism closely matches the definition of evaluation, in that the primary focus is to render a judgment. In fact, this practice should be labeled evaluation, except that it must be recognized that others in the field, especially accrediting bodies, refer to many of these practices as assessment, which is another example of the synonymous use of the terms. So although assessment for accountability is important, there also needs to be a focus on assessment for improvement, whether that improvement is on the individual, programmatic, or institutional level. This type of assessment tends to reflect new paradigm assumptions, such as discovering effectiveness in context, identifying patterns and tendencies (as opposed to focusing on predictability), interdependence, complexity, and growth from disorder (as opposed to only incremental improvement). With this type of assessment, data are generated about practice and outcomes and used to shape practice so that it is more effective. As will be seen in later discussions, adding this focus of assessment to the mix has an influence on the types of methods one might use to conduct assessment.

There is a paradox inherent in this dualism in that despite the realization and acceptance of complexity as the norm in new paradigm thinking, using learning and administrative outcomes to shape practice actually can be less complicated than assessment for accountability. For accountability purposes, a program or institution is frequently under pressure to obtain, discover, and document as many outcomes as possible to make a case for all that they are doing. Anyone involved with an institutional self-study process for the purpose of accreditation can attest to the reams of data generated about almost every conceivable outcome. However, when the purpose of assessment shifts to shaping practice, organizations can focus on a smaller number of sampled outcomes and shift the focus of the assessment to different practices as practice in one area improves. Another aspect of the paradox is that student affairs divisions that integrate ongoing practices of assessment to improve their everyday work will both generate a body of evidence related to effectiveness, and make a strong statement about their ability and likelihood to continue their growth and improvement.

## Problem-Generated Assessment and Development-Directed Assessment

The difference between these two forms of assessment is the source of the motivation for the assessment. In problem-generated assessment, a problem arises in practice resulting in stymied or lessened performance, or an individual or group is disappointed by the result of an action, that is, there is a problematic outcome. Problems can be as subtle as a misgiving about program direction or an individual's performance, or as significant and obvious as several resignations from a department in a short span of time or a sudden spike in student attrition. What each of these problems has in common is that the source of the motivation for assessment is external to any individual in the organization. It is the problem that stimulates the assessment activity, that is, data are collected about the situation and analyzed, actions are taken to address the problem, and, one hopes, performance improves. The individual or organization learns from this process for future situations.

However, development-directed assessment is internally motivated and operates under the assumption that learning and improvement are continuous. Assessment action is ongoing and includes situations in which there are no obvious problems or surprises. This type of assessment is generally part of the practice of individuals with an assessment mindset or organizations that have organizational learning as a core element of their culture. It is important to recognize the importance of both problem-based assessment and development-directed assessment.

### Assessment of Student Learning and Assessment of Practice

There also is the difference between two foci in the practice of assessment. There is the assessment that focuses on student learning outcomes and practices associated with those student learning outcomes and improving those outcomes, and the assessment that focuses on our administrative practice whether or not it is directly connected with student learning outcomes. Student learning outcomes include skills, knowledge, attitudes, and higher order thinking (for example, comprehension, application, analysis, synthesis, and evaluation). Administrative outcomes are virtually limitless and are related to the activities of management, budgeting, inventorying, information processing, information dissemination, communication, ordering, purchasing, and scheduling. These elements are separated because student affairs professionals are being encouraged and challenged to jump into the assessment of student learning outcomes for the purpose of enhancing those outcomes, yet many have not been conscious in the use of assessment in other more basic aspects of their jobs.

There are two steps that need to occur before the assessment of student learning outcomes can be effectively integrated into an organization's work. The first is the development of an assessment mindset as an individual professional, which is addressed in the next part of this chapter. The second is the incorporation and integration of assessment into administrative and professional practice for the purpose of improving service to and work with students and other stakeholders. To be effective and long-lasting, assessment cannot be an add-on to corporate practice, which represents old paradigm thinking of organizations as separate, fragmented pieces. Assessment must be an integral aspect of professional behavior.

## Assessment Mindset: Learning in and from Individual Practice

The assessment movement in which student affairs is currently immersed will have a more lasting impact on the field if individual professionals adopt an assessment mindset and if organizational learning is promoted as the core of an organization's culture. In this section the notion of an assessment mindset is addressed. An assessment mindset means that an individual's view of the world is one in which assessment is a filter that shapes that view of the world and the individual's experience in it. It means that individuals live the definition of assessment in their individual professional practice. That is, they consciously and intentionally gather, analyze, and interpret evidence that describes their individual effectiveness and use that evidence to improve their effectiveness. Senge et al. (1994) describe a deep learning cycle that is at the core of an assessment mindset:

Reflecting: Becoming an observer of one's own thinking and action

Connecting: Creating ideas and possibilities for action, and rearranging them into new forms

Deciding: Settling on a method for action

Doing: Performing a task, with as much of an experimental frame of mind as possible

There is a close parallel between this framework and Kolb's (1981) learning cycle: observations and reflections, abstract conceptualization, active experimentation, and concrete experience.

Professionals who practice this cycle of learning are not very difficult to find; however, many are probably not perceived or labeled as people with an "assessment mindset." Instead, as Donald Schön (1987) argued, they are usually viewed as individuals with wisdom or intuition or talent or inherent good judgment. The problem with labeling effective professionals with these very fine terms is that these labels, for the most part, imply that the skills, knowledge, and abilities they have are somehow inborn. It leads people to think that their effective skills and attributes blossomed due to the individuals' gaining enough years of experience, that is, their latent, natural talent became manifest with enough experience or being in the right position or institution or context. If this is actually the case, there is nothing to learn from these individuals, except patience to wait for one's own gifts to emerge and the hope one actually has these gifts.

The idea that skills are somehow genetic rather than learned is reinforced through conversations with such professionals about their assessment mindset, because for the most part the process through which they invoke the assessment mindset has become subconscious. Think of the entry-level professional who observes his supervisor handling a nasty interpersonal conflict that arises at a departmental meeting. The supervisor remains calm, not adding emotion to an already hot situation. She listens, she ensures that appropriate professional boundaries related to any conflict-related behavior are maintained, and she involves other staff members in mediating the conflict and in moving the group toward an appropriate resolution. She manages to do this with all members feeling they have been listened to and their concerns acknowledged and addressed. The entry-level person is very impressed with this display of professional poise and skill. Yet when he follows up with his supervisor to talk about the situation and how she came to have such skills, she thinks for a moment and says something like, "I've been through these situations before, I guess." This is not very helpful to the young professional, but it also is not a surprising response either. Asking her to either explain how she processed the action in the staff meeting or asking how she developed such a skill is akin to asking a professional quarterback how he knows how hard to throw a football to reach a receiver thirty yards downfield or asking the driver of an eighteen-wheel semi-tractor trailer the process she goes through to back into an alley off a busy city street with two feet to spare on either side. The typical and not very helpful response in both instances—"Practice!"

There is an important both-and aspect of an assessment mindset that goes beyond deep learning: the mindset is about both the past and the future. Merely living out the definition of assessment on an individual basis means that the individual's future is overly prescribed by the present and the past—what an individual is and will be doing will be an improved version of what that individual is currently doing and who she or he is now, which in turn was determined by past experiences and actions. To be an effective and creative professional, the future must be integrated with the mindset as well. So, it is not just about where someone is now and improving on that, but also where that person wants to be and identifying paths of living into that future. Individual assessment activities are focused on those professional elements that deal with planning and articulating a future vision for one's self, as well as the organization.

An assessment mindset can be consciously adopted to enhance one's professional practice and, in fact, given the increasing complexity of the world and work in student affairs, professionals must be more conscious about learning continuously and envisioning a future that will shape the present. Professionals' skill sets can and will drop from consciousness as they become ingrained; however, aspects of learning can and should remain conscious. This chapter represents the individual and organizational dynamic as well; it is another example of both-and. The individual needs to commit to conducting assessment in her or his own experience, but it becomes more powerful and effective when it is done in a culture of learning. An organization focused on learning and improving through assessment is more effective and future-oriented when enough individuals in the organization adopt an assessment mindset. An assessment mindset also goes hand-in-hand with aspects of pervasive leadership.

An assessment mindset—creating the future, assessing the present, defusing the past—is cultivated by an individual and not imposed through training. It does not just happen; it requires conscious practice. Reflective journaling and peer or supervisory debriefing can be important and helpful to the development of such a mindset.

## Assessment Mindset: Future, Present, and Past

When thinking about typical learning experiences, the temporal sequence most often is past-to-present-to-future. In fact, this is the way most people think about the direction of time in general. To determine what one needs to learn, most often a person begins with what she or he already knows or does not know (that is, what has been learned or failed to be learned in the past), which directs learning in the present, and shapes who the person will be in the future. In developing an assessment mindset, the sequence needs to be both past-to-present-to-future and future-to-present-to-past. Individuals need to begin with a view of a potential future for themselves; to do so, they work in the present on how to reach that future, and they defuse any past obstacles that keep them from progressing toward their chosen future. Although this is presented as a linear sequence of future-to-present-to-past, as individuals work on these elements of the mindset, they are eventually addressed concurrently. In fact, because the three time dimensions interact as a system, not only does the past influence the present and the future, but experiences in the present can help reshape and redefine the experience of the past. This latter experience happens all the time on an individual and organizational basis. A person develops an opinion of someone based on the individual's actions; yet as more is learned about the individual, the motivation for those actions and the actions themselves are seen in a different light, thus redefining the original experience. One need only think of a tough coach. During practice the actions of this individual are often viewed negatively. It is usually after the fact that the actions are reframed and one's perception of the individual is redefined as well. A real life organizational example of redefining the past from the perspective of the present is New York University's investment activities during the 1990s. In many quarters this university was the laughing stock of competitors in the higher education world because of its conservative investment strategies. Yet following the collapse of the economy in the late 1990s, those conservative strategies came to be viewed in a different and more positive light, since they allowed NYU to better weather the economic storm than some of their peer institutions (Pulley, 2002).

## Personal Vision: Living into the Future

Beginning with the future is not about predicting where one will be in five years, nor is it about putting on blinders and a straightjacket and slavishly pursuing one particular future or goal. Instead, this is about contemplating the future and choosing one possible future to direct present activities. Again, this particular part of the competency is called a mindset, not a plan. Part of having an assessment mindset is to be freed from the constraints of the past. A person begins to do that by contemplating the future. Covey (1989, p. 97), in *The Seven Habits of Highly Effective People*, speaks about "beginning with the end in mind." It is the fact that a person creates a vision, not what the vision is; the fact that someone is choosing a future to live into, not the fact that he or she may or may not ultimately experience that particular future. As Senge, et al. (1994, p. 195) point out, "There are many stories of people who achieve extraordinary results with extraordinary visions—where the results happen to be different from their original intent."

A personal vision needs to address the issues and concerns of personal and professional importance. It needs to be about who a person will be, not what that individual will do. Developing a powerful personal vision forces a person to come to terms with what is personally valued, the principles one aspires to live by, and those areas of one's professional life that one might desire to change. A personal vision should become an instrument used to focus priorities. It is a choice for a particular future and it becomes a guidepost for subsequent choices. By constructing and choosing a personal vision a person is making a commitment to creating the results one wants. To be effective, the vision needs to be assimilated into one's daily life. It is not a set of goals, and cannot sit in a desk drawer. Nor is a personal vision the same thing as a professional philosophy, which is a set of values and beliefs related to one's professional practice. Values and beliefs exist in the present and are rooted in the past. They often may guide the choice of a personal vision, but in themselves are not a personal vision.

A personal vision inspires action in the present; it does not predict outcomes or even specify action. Instead, a vision acts as strange attractor. So like the organizational vision described in pervasive leadership, a personal vision can shape action and lead to patterns in behavior, but it does not determine behavior, nor does it predict the outcome of actions taken in pursuit of the vision. In addition, one of the results of constructing a personal vision is that one takes responsibility for that choice and the actions taken to live into that future. The individual loses the ability to put total blame on the past or on others for one's current situation.

## Assessment in Action: Learning from the Present

Typically, an individual's present is merely an extension of that person's past—past learning, past successes, past experiences, past perspectives. In the present a person does what she or he has done, hopefully better, but usually similar to what she or he has done in the past. By inserting the future into the idea of an assessment mindset, a present is created that now includes a tension between what has been done in the past and the future that has been chosen. Senge et al. (1994) speak of a creative tension that exists between the present and a future guided by a personal vision. However, the source of the tension is really the past's influence on the present. Senge et al. depict the tension through the image of stretching a rubber band between one's hands—one hand represents the vision, the other represents the present. A third hand and a second rubber band need to be added—the vision is pulling the present forward into the future, but the past is holding the present back as a continuation of the past. People struggle to live into the future they have chosen for themselves, but the past is holding them back. Releasing the past's "rubber band" is the subject of the next section—defusing obstacles.

It is in the present that people participate in the learning activities that form the core of any assessment practice. One of the first things to discover is where one is vis-à-vis the personal vision. Again, the typical pattern of assessment behavior is to assess where one is, and based on what is discovered, determine where to go and what to do. This means that the future is being overdetermined by the present and the past, when the assessed actions took place. Instead, in an assessment mindset, it is the future that determines the central focus of the assessment. If someone has a vision of being a speaker of Chinese in the future, that person needs to assess just how much Chinese she or he currently knows. If an individual has a vision of being a leader in the field of student affairs, she or he needs to assess her or his leadership skills and experiences, and the outcomes of leadership experiences. Not only does a person need to assess where they are in relationship to their vision, but they also need to assess how much of their current practice relates to their vision. To repeat the previous example, if a person has a vision of being a leader in the field of student affairs, she or he also needs to assess how much of what they are doing currently relates to that vision and the possibility of fulfilling that vision.

It is in the present where the lens of assessment is consciously and intentionally focused on the individual and individual practice, where evidence is gathered, analyzed, and interpreted, and where that evidence is used to improve individual effectiveness. Brown (1991, p. 125) referred to this as having "an ethos of inquiry," where one's mindset is focused on collecting data and evidence regarding practice, searching for explanations for what appears in the data and evidence collected in a particular setting, examining research from other sources and practices in other settings, and improving practice by using these data. Pascarella and Whitt (1999) identify a practice they refer to as systematic inquiry—the intentional, organized, and ongoing search for information. They focus their attention on practices related to the enhancement of student learning outcomes, but the principles they present can be applied to individual practice as well. What they add beyond what Brown indicated is the importance of knowing what has already been researched and discovered about the practices and issues in question. Student affairs professionals need to be aware of the knowledge that already exists in the field and compare what one is doing to what appears to be effective in other settings.

An assessment mindset also involves bringing the past into the present for the purpose of conscious and intentional examination. Professionals must ask, What happened? Why did that happen? How did that happen? How effective was it? How does what happened relate to what I did or did not do? How can I change what I do to bring about different, more effective results? This does not require, though it does not discount, formal data collection. It requires a willingness, openness, and commitment to examining past actions and the apparent results of action. Whereas reflection is bringing the past into the present, one also needs to push the present into the future. This is done by planning and experimenting, actively pursuing a vision, trying different things, using the data, analysis, and reflection activities to suggest other actions that might be taken, and then taking them. This continues the cycle of learning that is at the heart of the assessment mindset, developing a simple plan of action and then experimenting with it.

### Defusing Obstacles: Putting the Past in the Past

Obstacles are those things that try to keep the present rooted solely in the past. They influence the present and keep people from living their personal visions. The initial label for this section was "dismantling obstacles." We started with the idea that to move confidently into the future, one needs to dismantle the obstacles that bind her or him to the past. However, to dismantle something is to break it apart, to destroy it. That type of action takes a tremendous amount of energy and usually quite a bit of time. In the case of dismantling obstacles to the future, one would be focusing this energy on the past, when the energy and time needs to be focused on the future. Instead, we came to realize it is not necessary to destroy the obstacles, only to bracket and defuse them. Although bracketing and defusing an obstacle may leave it intact, it removes the obstacle's power to influence us. This requires much less energy than dismantling obstacles.

There are many obstacles to effective professional practice. However, the obstacles most salient when developing an assessment mindset are internal, not external. The most powerful internal obstacles are the assumptions individuals hold about themselves ("There's nothing I can do anyway"), their roles ("It's not my job"), and the issues they face ("That's beyond my control"). Assumptions are vital to human communication, human organization, and human interpersonal relationships. They are the taken-for-granted beliefs that guide an individual's action; and when they are shared within a group of people (albeit subconsciously), they guide actions in organizations and form the basis of the organization's culture.

Assumptions are subconscious; they influence behavior without individuals being aware assumptions are influencing their behavior. In fact, the power that most assumptions have over people *is* their subconscious nature. If they remain subconscious, the accuracy of the assumption cannot be examined; people act as though it is true. Bringing assumptions to the surface, to consciousness, exposes them to the possibility of analysis and reflection. If such an analysis results in the discovery of a false assumption (for example, "I guess I really do have leadership abilities"), that assumption drops and is replaced by a different, more empowering assumption (for example, "I am a leader"). Identifying assumptions is the prime focus of defusing obstacles to developing an assessment mindset, especially those assumptions that are disempowering and those that contribute to ineffective practice. An assessment mindset goes beyond testing and improving practice, it also requires questioning the axioms held about practice, staff, peers, students, supervisors, and one's institution. This is the root of the difference between single-loop and double-loop learning (Argyris & Schön, 1974). Single-loop learning is applying feedback and learning to the task at hand. In double-loop learning, assumptions underlying current practices are discovered and questioned, and hypotheses about the practices are tested publicly and consciously (Argyris, 1976). In single loop learning, someone can identify better ways to run a staff meeting. In double-loop learning, the individual questions why there are staff meetings. What is accomplished? Are there other ways to achieve the same ends? Identifying obstacles to an assessment mindset should involve interrogating ingrained practices, assumptions about oneself, what a person is capable of, and what one knows or does not know. One can begin this process of assumption discovery by noticing when something is a surprise. Being surprised means that something has happened that was not expected. It also means that the individual had an expectation—an assumption— that something else would happen.

Adopting an assessment mindset might be the most important challenge presented in this book. With it, the rest of the book is read from the perspective of learning and from the perspective of the future one seeks to live into, the future an individual wishes to lead her or his organization into. Adopting an assessment mindset requires persistence, patience, and the willingness to actively and consciously reflect on one's experience. Of course, adopting or enhancing such a mindset is much easier in a supportive organizational context, an organizational context based in and focused on organizational learning.

## Organizational Learning

Looking at assessment from a both-and perspective leads to addressing both the individual and the organizational dimensions of assessment. This section focuses on organizational learning because, in addition to addressing competencies or practices of assessment, one must also consider the organizational context through which assessment is conducted. From a Newtonian organization perspective, assessment is rather simple—collect data to improve specific processes. From a new science perspective, one needs to consider the complexity of the practice of assessment.

*Organizational learning* is the collective process through which future states are envisioned and knowledge about current organizational assumptions, processes, and outcomes related to those future states is acquired and applied so that those processes and outcomes are improved to better contribute to the success of the organization and the creation of the desired future. Organizational learning is a broad, deep, and complex topic, so only those aspects of organizational learning that relate most closely with our notions of an assessment mindset and assessment practice are addressed—group learning and systems thinking. Senge (2000) speaks of three core organizational learning competencies:

- Aspiration toward learning, growing, and addressing issues of importance

- Reflective conversation as a way to discover assumptions and ways of seeing

- Understanding complexity within organizations

The first two issues are addressed through a focus on group learning and the third by discussing the concept of systems thinking. This section concludes with a discussion about *closing the loop*, the art and practice of applying knowledge, evidence, and information in a new situation.

All organizations are learning organizations if they have managed to exist for more than a few years. That is, most organizations have learned from and adapted to internal and external stimuli, crises, changing trends, and so forth. However, the notion of a learning organization involves bringing these learning processes to a conscious level to make them more effective and to overcome barriers to effective learning. Learning organizations move beyond adaptive learning, a reactive form of learning, to more proactive and future-focused forms of learning described in the definition of organizational learning in the preceding paragraph. The idea of bringing assumptions and processes to a conscious level is not a new concept. For example, on the individual level, bringing the subconscious into consciousness is one of the key aspects of double-loop learning (Argyris & Schön, 1974). However, at the organizational level bringing the subconscious into consciousness is a much more important, but often avoided, process.

### Assessment and Group Learning

An assessment mindset is about individual learning and assessment for improvement. To most effectively transform organizational assessment practices into organizational learning, the information and data that are collected in organizational assessment processes must be fed back into the system in multiple places to enhance the functioning of the organization. Ultimately, assessment is about the learning that is produced—learning on the part of students, but also learning on the part of the organization. Earlier, it was stated that assessment is about learning. It is also true that organizational learning is at least in part about assessment.

Senge et al. (1994) assert that a deep learning cycle constitutes the essence of a learning organization—the fundamental shifts of mind, individually and collectively. Group learning is dependent upon individual learning and the assessment mindset, and vice versa. To have effective and lasting change take place, managers need to find a way to tap into this rhythm—to create not only time to think, but also time for different types of thought and collective discussion. Although there is often individual learning without group learning, there is no group learning without individual learning. The root of group learning *is* individual learning. Senge et al. (1994) describe a group equivalent for the deep learning cycle for individuals (that is, reflecting, connecting, deciding, and doing). At the organizational level, the reflection stage is "public reflection" because the observation of thinking and action takes place in a common space and is open to the scrutiny of others. When individual reflection becomes public and conscious, it opens the possibility of consensus, commonality, and mutual understanding. The connecting stage equivalent for the group is "shared meaning" where the creation and construction of ideas and possibilities for action are conducted as a group. Shared meaning is followed by "joint planning" or joint design. Finally, there is "coordinated action," which need not be joint action. This means that various members of the organization, who may work in different functions and locations, can carry the action out independently. This "wheel of learning" is the heart of organizational learning. Senge, et al. point out that it is the public reflection and shared meaning stages that are often skipped. It is not surprising, given the concern over the lack of individual and organizational assessment in student affairs, that the processes of public reflection and shared meaning are those most associated with the notion of assessment. It is during these phases that data are collected from the result of the coordinated action, analyzed, discussed, and fed back into the system to enhance the process and the result outcomes during the next cycle.

### Assessment and Systems Thinking

Effective organizational learning requires a great appreciation for complexity in organizational functioning, and system dynamics is one way in which complexity is described in organizational functioning. Senge, et al. (1994) describe a system as "a perceived whole whose elements 'hang together' because they continually affect each other over time and operate toward a common purpose" (p. 90). Systems are separate entities that possess idiosyncratic, dynamic, and unique properties separate and apart from their subunits. Examples of systems include biological organisms, the atmosphere, communities, teams, and organizations. Individuals are part of many different systems—the organization within which a person works, family, community, neighborhood, and so forth. From a systems perspective, a sports team is an entity separate and apart from and more than a group of players. Systems cannot be separated from their environment, and all systems are recognized as being open, that is, the boundaries of the system are not barriers and are in effect arbitrary, even if everyone agrees upon where the boundaries are. For example, how does an individual define the boundaries of one's family? Is it siblings and parents? Does it include grandparents, aunts, and uncles? What about cousins? What about non-blood related people who are called brother or sister? The boundaries of any organizational system are just as arbitrary. Systems thinking is grounded in the assumptions of the new paradigm; a system goes well beyond the independent, fragmented, and discrete units described by the traditional paradigm.

System dynamics are the mutually shaping patterns "of interrelationships among key components of the system. That might include the hierarchy and process flows, but it also includes attitudes and perceptions, the quality of products, the ways in which decisions are made, and various other factors" (Senge et al., 1994, p. 90). Systems thinking is the epitome of recognizing connectedness described in the first chapter. The structure of any system is also in continuous dynamic flux. The structure involves not just the elements of the system—in the case of the family example, the people in the family—but also the evolving relationships among them, as well as how those relationships change in the presence of other system elements. A person may interact with a sibling very differently when another sibling is there.

An example of systems thinking on the part of an individual, albeit often done subconsciously, is driving in traffic. A driver on a busy highway is in relationship with all the other cars on the highway and is responding to the action of each car in the immediate vicinity, and in some cases responsively anticipating the actions of a driver directly ahead by the actions of the driver in front of him or her (for example, removing one's foot from the accelerator and placing it over the brake when a car up ahead suddenly veers into one's lane, cutting off the car ahead). In busy conditions, one also is observing the overall system and structure of traffic. As volume increases, periodic slowdowns are anticipated. Seeing brake lights far ahead leads to taking one's foot off the accelerator and anticipating the need to brake, but in the meantime also slowing down and affecting other cars. A driver cannot predict when the slowdowns will occur but can recognize the pattern, which in effect contributes to creating the pattern anticipated (that is, starting to slow down). Also, the boundaries of the traffic are porous with multiple on and off ramps.

The structure of a system depends on the perception and filter through which it is observed, so the system is not just what is there, but how it is interpreted by the observer. Systems thinking requires the ability to see the "bigger picture" and the myriad of small pictures that makes up the big picture, that is, the ability to recognize the complex interplay of organizational elements and their influence on organizational outcomes. It is our argument that part of the frustration in assessing for accountability is that it does not adequately take into consideration the complexity of organizational action and interaction that eventually results in the outcomes being measured. Those who focus solely on accountability aspire to reduce administrative and learning outcomes to simple measures. In addition, such outcomes, typically in some form of numeric data, tend not to provide clues as to how to improve the outcomes. As an organization grows in appreciation for the complexity of organizational functioning and seeks to better understand that complexity, more and more assessment activities will shift to assessment for improvement.

Adding to the complexity is the fact that systems are not reducible to simple cause and effect relationships, which is an old paradigm assumption. It is difficult, and often impossible, to directly link individual job performance to the achievement of organizational goals. This is why it is important to focus on processes, strategies, and actions, not just outcomes. John Spencer (2000), a senior research specialist in the Office of Student Life Studies at the University of Missouri–Columbia, provides a good example of the frustration that results from the old paradigm aspirations for simplicity and predictability. After programs in the Division of Student Affairs focused for a year on enhancing student success, the graduation rates and mean student grade point average (GPA), which are measurable outcomes, both rose. However, even with efforts redoubled the next year, the same measures fell. Frustration resulted, which further suppressed effective organizational action. In a relatively short time, it appeared to members of the organization that incorporating assessment, albeit assessment for accountability, into organizational behavior resulted in a decline in organizational effectiveness. By focusing only on the 'bottom line' and not considering the complexity of reaching that bottom line, staff became frustrated with the lack of control they felt. Before assessment they believed they were contributing to the bottom line. However, during the time that they focused on assessment for accountability, they became convinced that their work had no influence on the bottom line. Although he did not label it as such, Spencer (2000) described a shift toward assessment for improvement along with a recognition of the complex integrated system of organizational action that contributed to the bottom line. The programs within the division were encouraged to reduce their emphasis on measuring global outcomes (for example, GPA and graduation rates) as an indication of their level of effectiveness and instead focused on assessing and analyzing local strategies, actions, and outcomes related to their program's goals and vision. Spencer (2000) goes on to describe the more effective local *and* global outcomes resulting from this shift in assessment focus. From the perspective of systems thinking, Spencer convinced the units to focus on the elements of the system, not just the system itself.

## Closing the Loop: The Critical Learning Connection

Filling the gap between evidence (that is, knowledge, information, data, understanding) about what we are doing and actions taken in response to the evidence is what we refer to as *closing the loop*, that is, the feedback loop. Systems thinking is very sensitive to the notion of feedback loops; they are part of the dynamic interrelationships that exist throughout a system. In fact, feedback loops are what causes a great deal of the dynamism in a system. Komives (2000) spoke of closing the loop in reference to helping individual students take meaningful and thoughtful action in their lives in response to the knowledge and understanding available to them. In fact, she argued that it is a prime responsibility of student affairs professionals to "inhabit the gap" and help students bridge knowledge to action. The same challenge holds true for learning and acting in and as organizations. Many individuals and organizations recognize the knowledge of effective practice; however, often they have not committed to incorporating that knowledge into practice, and they have not created the space for the actions that would require. Organizational learning requires examining individually and organizationally espoused values and priorities and determining the degree to which they are utilized in individual and organizational lives. Closing the loop requires intentionality, an assessment mindset, and an awareness of the individual and organizational learning processes.

## Assessment Practice

This section addresses aspects of the assessment movement as it has been experienced in student affairs. Although this is based on traditional notions of assessment practice in extant literature, approaching it from the perspective of an assessment mindset and organizational learning will create a different understanding and will result in action different from those of traditional, old-science assumptions of organizational behavior. Three sets of principles are described that establish a foundation for effective assessment. The sets are labeled organizational context, procedural assumptions for effective assessment, and assessment in action. This section is written from the perspective of assessment at the level of organization; however, individual professionals can seek starting points for their own organizational unit, or ideas they could use to start conversations within their unit about the need to incorporate assessment as a means to positively influence organizational performance.

### Organizational Context

Using assessment to shape organizational and individual practice needs to occur within a supportive organizational context. These five principles suggest an approach that will lead to such a supportive context.

- Align assessment plans and the outcomes in question with institutional purpose and mission. Effective assessment plans flow from the institutional mission and values. This refers both to the formal mission—where one is available, clear, and specific—and to the "lived" mission, based upon in-depth knowledge and practices of the institution. Just as a personal vision identifies a future the individual is living into, the institutional mission needs to identify the ends and outcomes expected for the many clients of the institution, especially students. The mission needs to avoid a focus on activities and aspirations and instead focus on ends and futures (Carver, 2000). Personal visions of individual organizational members should be consonant with the institutional mission. Assessment practice should focus on questions that constituents believe to be the most important and that will result in information to assist in improving individual, programmatic, and institutional performance and helping the organization live into the future as defined by the vision. Assessment plans should provide explicit and public statements and goals about institutional values and expectations for student learning and administrative practice.

- Link assessment plans to the division's and the institution's strategic planning process. Assessment cannot be a separate, stand-alone process. It must be part of the organizational system and integrated with planning and other activities in the division and institution. Assessment processes need to be conscious and public, so that institutional constituencies are aware of and can react to and participate in the planning and implementation process. Wherever possible, student affairs assessment plans and processes should be integrated into institutional planning.

- Recruit leadership from senior administrators and commitment from institutional members. Leadership in assessment is vital, yet a top-down-only process will have difficulty succeeding. Assessment is an aspect of organizational functioning in which pervasive leadership is crucial. A critical mass of institutional members—members with assessment mindsets—must be committed to and provide leadership for the assessment process and the use of assessment data to shape individual and organizational practice.

- Partner with others to implement effective assessment efforts. Student affairs professionals need to recognize the importance of spanning boundaries and working with faculty, academic administrators, other institutional administrators, and off-campus constituents in seeking to implement organizational assessment practices. Ideally, academic and student affairs professionals should advance and jointly assess institutionwide learning outcomes as well as the organizational practices linked to those outcomes. However, failure to have such a relationship should not deter student affairs professionals from instituting their own processes. Student affairs assessment efforts may be the small fluctuation in the overall system that could lead to dramatic change in the future.

- Invest divisional and institutional resources in the assessment process. Assessing outcomes as a step toward program and administrative improvement is not something that can merely be added to the staff's workload. It will require time, space, personnel, and funds. Designating resources specifically for assessment will clearly communicate commitment to the assessment process. Yet having inadequate resources is not a reason to fail to incorporate assessment into individual and organizational practice.

## Procedural Assumptions

A number of aspects of the assessment process need to be considered during the planning and implementation phase. These procedural assumptions help guide effective integration of assessment into everyday practice.

- Effective assessment is ongoing, not episodic. Effective assessment is not merely an aspect of an annual evaluation process; it is integrated into one's work, hence the notion of an assessment mindset. Assessment at the programmatic and institutional level is evolutionary, continuous, and incremental. A division of student affairs would be wise to begin with encouraging the development of an assessment mindset among its constituents and with modest organizational assessment efforts; over time, the efforts can become more comprehensive, systemic, and integrative. Assessment plans and related processes need to be regularly reviewed, evaluated, revised, and aligned with the division's and institution's mission.

- Assessment plans specify both outcomes a priori and identify unanticipated outcomes. Specifying outcomes, especially in the form of setting goals and establishing expectations grounded in the organizational vision, ahead of time helps direct one's efforts. It is what Angelo (1995) meant by making expectations explicit and public. However, given the complexity of higher education, unanticipated positive and negative outcomes will occur. Assessment plans and processes need to acknowledge and seek out these unanticipated outcomes. In the terminology of chaos theory, these are fluctuations. As unanticipated outcomes are discovered, the enhancement of the positive outcomes and diminution of the negative outcomes can be included in future rounds of planning and become a priori outcomes.

- Assessment processes vary and reflect the distinct character of each organization and institution. Assessment plans and processes cannot be imported from other institutions and applied directly to a new context. Given the uniqueness of any organizational entity, assessment plans or processes from beyond the boundaries of a unit must be examined through the history, perspectives, personnel, and experiences of that particular organizational unit. Assessment efforts need to be grown within the organizational system, not added onto it.

- Effective assessment plans are multidimensional. Part of the multidimensional nature of assessment is the recognition of the complexity of learning and administrative processes. Assessment efforts should collect both quantitative and qualitative data. Data can and should be collected from multiple constituents and stakeholders, such as staff, prospective students, current students, alumni, and alumnae to provide information and data from multiple perspectives. The process can involve different data gathering instruments and methods, such as actual performance, individual interviews, focus groups, standardized tests, locally constructed or national tests and surveys, portfolios, and licensure exams. Databases, data collection devices, and processes already in use can and should be incorporated into the division's assessment practices.

- Shaping practice in response to the assessment of student learning outcomes most often requires cultural transformation of the organizational unit and, when fully implemented, results in cultural transformation of the unit. This organizational dynamic is another example of a paradox and both-and. Not surprising, the culture of the status quo is more powerful than change efforts focused on assessment and quality improvement. The creation and implementation of an organizational plan for assessment must include actions to consciously counter the aspects of the organization's culture that will resist the changes needed for effective implementation. Tying individual reward systems and departmental budgets to assessment efforts places positive pressure on the change process. The internal obstacles to an assessment mindset described earlier form part of the cultural resistance to assessment efforts. Yet when enough obstacles are removed and assessment practice is instituted, other underlying assumptions, values, and norms of the organization's culture will be transformed as well.

## Assessment in Action

The following principles address the process of using learning and administrative outcomes to shape professional practice.

- Assessment needs to focus both on process and outcomes. As Pike (2000) emphasized, outcome measures will provide information on what is happening but may not provide the necessary information needed to improve the outcomes. Instead, strategies, processes, and actions also must be assessed and understood if improvement is to be managed and encouraged. Focusing on processes as well as outcomes will help in identifying strategies to "close the loop."

- Assessment must be organizationally pervasive. For maximum effectiveness, assessment needs to be promoted and coordinated, thus implying traditional leadership emanating from high in the organization. However, the process of assessment must also pervade the organization. Assessment and especially the collection of data cannot be left solely to a student affairs assessment office. This is why developing an assessment mindset among organizational members is vital. The data must be collected *and* analyzed as close to the source of action as possible, as well as fed back to the entire organization.

- Continuous improvement is an integral aspect of assessment. All knowledge gained from assessment is contingent, because improvement is always possible and change for the better is always in view although not yet attained. Assessment should result in the alteration or elimination of activities when analyses indicate changes are desirable. Results of assessment processes should be compared to previous outcomes within the organization as well as to external organizations similar to one's own and recognized to have excellent or comparable outcomes. This latter practice is known as benchmarking.

- Outcomes of assessment are used to shape practice at multiple levels of the institution. This is perhaps the most important aspect of assessment for improvement, and it is what truly distinguishes assessment for improvement from assessment for accountability. The audience interested in accountability is typically external to the site of the assessment. They can be outside of the site but internal to the organization, such as reporting results to administration, or they can be external to the entire organization (for example, an accrediting body). The audience interested in improvement is the organizational unit itself. Clear communication channels back to units are essential to ensure the results are used to improve practice related to student learning outcomes or administrative practice at multiple levels of the organization. Changes in administrative practice, pedagogy, curriculum, co-curriculum, and academic support services resulting from the analysis and feedback of assessment data must be documented and communicated broadly on campus to continue and reinforce the learning and improvement aspects of assessment.

## Getting Started

One of the stumbling blocks often cited by individuals and organizations seeking to incorporate assessment into their work is being unsure how to get started. Individuals can shape the following suggestions to meet their needs, or use them as a starting point for conversation within their particular organization.

- Implement training. Prior to planning any assessment effort, individuals, departments, and divisions need to be adequately trained and share a common language and understanding of the assessment process. The training should focus on developing an assessment mindset, group learning, and systems thinking, as well as traditional skills associated with assessment, such as interviewing, survey construction, other data collection techniques, and data analysis.

- Establish or clarify the student affairs mission. The mission of student affairs needs to be a living document that creates one possible future for the division, drives planning, goal-setting, and practice, and serves as a benchmark against which practice is compared. To this end, staff intent on shaping their practice in response to the assessment of administrative and student learning outcomes must establish, review, clarify, or revise their mission with this purpose in mind.

- Establish learning as a nonnegotiable goal of the division. Obviously, such a commitment must emanate from the top of the division and be incorporated into the mission of the division. This goal encompasses student learning, staff learning, individual learning, group learning, and organizational learning.

- Identify initial areas of focus. The initial focus of an assessment effort needs to be areas important to multiple stakeholders. The effort must garner a significant level of investment from organizational members for it to be successful and if it is to serve as the foundation from which a more comprehensive assessment effort will grow. Any planning effort should identify and include those for whom this is an important issue, as well as any constituent group affected by the assessment process.

- Focus on what is important, not just easy to measure. Focus on areas important to multiple stakeholders. Unfortunately, departments and divisions often focus on what is easy to measure (for example, program attendance, retention, GPAs) and hope these can serve as proxies for what is important. If focusing on what is important was easy, organizations would already be doing it. When individual, organizational, and student learning is established as the primary goal of the division, more pressure will be brought to bear on assessing learning on multiple levels (Pike, 2000).

- Involve key players. In addition to members of constituent groups affected by the assessment effort, other key players need to be involved in the assessment planning and process, including faculty, academic administrators, members of the administration, and alumni and alumnae.

- Consider the political consequences of any assessment effort. Any assessment effort has a strong political dimension. Although shaping practice often means learning how to improve current efforts and performance, it could result in a decision to shift resources, personnel, and emphasis, or even to create or eliminate programs. The political consequences should be considered from the outset. Focusing on improvement over accountability, expecting pervasive participation, and focusing on process as well as outcomes will somewhat ameliorate, though not eliminate, potentially harmful political consequences.

- Identify a champion. Leadership is required both from top administrators and members throughout the organization. Assessment efforts need to be highly collaborative ventures; however, each assessment effort should have an identifiable champion. This individual or group of individuals will go beyond the normal actions of a chairperson and become an advocate, cheerleader, and organizer. The champion will overcome obstacles and remove barriers to the overall assessment effort.

---

Assessment is much more than traditional notions of evaluation. In fact, assessment as conceived in this chapter is grounded in the individual's view of the world, hence the notion of an assessment mindset. Someone with an assessment mindset is more likely to seek to conduct assessment for purposes of improvement (over accountability), generate assessment for development (as opposed to in response to problems), and assess both administrative practices and student learning outcomes. In addition, the primary focuses of assessment should be drawn from the future (that is, the vision of the individual, the organization, or both), rather than strictly from the past (that is, assessing what is being done now and has been done in the past). Assessment plans, programs, and practices are then much more effective when they are conducted by individuals who work from an assessment mindset and in an organization focused on organizational learning. The main point of this chapter is that assessment understood from a new science perspective is a complex, multidimensional process—not a linear one. Recognizing this should liberate professionals, not intimidate them. One should just begin to do it, and expect surprises along the way. Like intrapreneurship, one needs to be open to the feedback that is received in the process. These perspectives and those from the previous chapters form a foundation for the competencies addressed in the rest of this book: resource awareness, enhancement, and attraction; technology; adoption of a global perspective, and futures forecasting.

# Part II

# Seeing Resources Differently
## *What We Work With*

Part Two (Chapters Five and Six) shifts from the "how" or processes of student affairs work to the "what" of student affairs work or, in other words, the resources used to accomplish that work. No work can be purely about processes, which describe actions. The processes work on, through, and use resources. This dynamic is an overarching example of both-and: student affairs work requires and involves both processes and resources. Student affairs professionals spend more time considering processes than they do resources, in part because they use a narrow definition of resources. So student affairs professionals need both to think more about and rethink resources.

Chapter Five, "Rethinking Resources," focuses on the ideas of resources awareness, resource enhancement, and resource attraction. Enhancing resource awareness requires adopting a broader definition of resource, whose basic definition is a source of supply, support, or aid, either actively being used or held in reserve. The chapter presents arguments that beyond traditionally considered resources of money, space, time, and personnel, there are resources such as information, relationships, expertise, and experience. Resource enhancement involves renewing, growing, and converting current resources. It is also about maximizing and making most effective use of available resources. Resource attraction focuses on ways to draw additional resources into the organization. The attraction methods described in the chapter are fundraising, grant writing, and partnerships. It is expected that rethinking resources as described in the chapter will enhance the effectiveness of the processes of student affairs work.

Chapter Six, "Technology as Brush, Paint, and Artist," focuses on one particular and increasingly pervasive resource—technology. The title of the chapter refers to the fact that technology is a tool to assist in work (brush), it is a medium shaped by professionals and through which work is accomplished (paint), and it is the technological skills and mindset of the individual professional brought to bear on the problems and issues in student affairs work (artist). The chapter does not share specific technological information on hardware or software; instead it suggests a particular mindset and a set of perspectives with which professionals can rethink the role of technology in their work.

# 5

# Rethinking Resources

Part One focused on some of the processes of student affairs practice, specifically leadership and assessment. It included the notion of intrapreneurship, described as pervasive leadership in action. Practice and action are predicated on the use of resources; that is, all processes require resources. Processes and resources are interconnected; one needs both effective processes and adequate resources in order to produce high-quality outcomes. This chapter focuses on resources in general; the next addresses the emergent resource of technology.

The primary purpose of this chapter is to challenge student affairs professionals to rethink the concept of resources. A resource is a source of supply, support, or aid, either actively being used or held in reserve. Resources are organizational and individual assets and the lifeblood through which day-to-day jobs are accomplished and through which new endeavors are attempted. To be *resourceful* describes someone who is inventive, creative, clever, and adaptable. So resources are assets allowing organizational members to invent, adapt, be clever, and create. Specifically, this chapter addresses *resource awareness*, which is becoming aware of the wide variety of resources at play in work; *resource enhancement*, which is growing and making better use of the resources an organization has; and *resource attraction*, which involves bringing new resources into the division.

Most universities deal with the issue of financial constraints. This has been especially true since the collapse in the mid–1970s of higher education's post-World War II Golden Era when there was tremendous financial support from federal and state governments. The latter part of the 1970s and the decade of the 1980s saw support flatten and decline. The nadir was the recession of the late 1980s, when even states with long histories of support for higher education, especially Massachusetts, New York, and California, dramatically cut subsidies for public higher education. Private institutions saw an even more dramatic shift from grants and scholarships to loans for students. The 1990s witnessed a never-before-seen decade-long economic expansion, yet many institutions continued to experience constrained resources. It is not surprising then that financial constraints are even more true today, as universities continue to deal with the fallout from the dot-com collapse, the general economic downturn, and continuing repercussions of the boardroom and accounting scandals in the private sector. Coupled with these issues is the intensifying pressure to rein in tuition increases, especially when considering that during the decade of the 1990s tuition for public colleges rose an average of 22 percent and tuition for private colleges rose 28 percent (U.S. Department of Education, 1999).

Beyond institutional concerns, constrained resources traditionally have been a challenge for many student affairs divisions. Although it is true that the proportion of institutional resources dedicated to student affairs divisions has not decreased in the last forty years (Woodard et al., 2000), these divisions have been asked to take on more tasks and mandates (for example, Americans with Disabilities Act compliance, crime statistics reporting). Advice for professionals often comes in the form of clichés, such as "you will need to do more with less" or in this case, "much more with about the same." Woodard et al. (2000) point out that working in an environment of constrained resources has the inevitable consequence of individuals squelching ideas before they reach full consciousness. Individuals learn "not to waste their own individual resources (for example, time to think, consider, dream, or plan) on notions that are dead ends" (p. 97).

The most common response to fiscal challenges has been to tighten financial controls. Other typical strategies used in higher education are making across-the-board budget cuts, maintaining hiring freezes, prohibiting out-of-state travel, deferring maintenance, slashing budgets for particular units, and setting new rules for budgeting. In addition, institutions are turning to outsourcing as one method for dealing with resource issues. Dining services, bookstores, health and medical services, security, and even residence halls are examples of student services privatized on many campuses during the past several decades. Some institutions are going beyond these to other, more core student affairs areas. An example is the City Colleges of Chicago, the city's community colleges, which replaced their academic counselors with college advisors supplied by an outside firm (Evelyn, 2002). Student affairs divisions deal with resource constraints in several of the same ways as institutions do. They institute across-the-board budget cuts, defer maintenance, slash budgets for particular units, and set new rules for budgeting. In response to this climate, attracting additional revenues, especially through fund-raising, is an emergent practice in student affairs (Penney & Rose, 2001).

Iannozzi believes that the solution to diminishing funding is to "broaden and diversify sources of revenue by renegotiating the culture of the institution to become more strategic in its planning activities, revenue allocation, and engagement of internal and external constituencies" (2002, p. 2). Changing the culture of an institution, and student affairs in particular, begins with individual professionals seeing elements of their work differently. Student affairs professionals need to become more cognizant of the role of resources in their work and more cognizant of their role as enhancers and attractors of resources. Traditional notions and definitions of educator or counselor or academic advisor do not include resource attractor or fund raiser as aspects of that job, therefore, many professionals resist accepting them as part of their job. Student affairs professionals need to move beyond limiting labels or limited definitions of these labels in order to become the intrapreneurs discussed in Chapter Three. Creativity will be limited and constrained until student affairs professionals see their world through a resource lens. When individuals adopt a resource awareness perspective they are more likely to be mindful of many more possible sources of resources.

## Resource Categories

Resources can be categorized in a variety of ways. The following categories differentiate among resources in an organization. The examples listed are described in the section on resource awareness.

- *Renewable*. The resource can be used again, generated again, or grown. It can also be saved, or held in reserve. Examples described below include people, information, relationships, and expertise.

- *Nonrenewable savable*. The resource can be used once but then it is gone. It can also be reserved for the time it is needed. Examples include supplies, basic services, and training materials.

- *Nonrenewable nonsavable*. The resource can be used or not used, either way it is gone and cannot be recovered. Examples include time and space.

- *Resource generating*. The resource can be used to generate additional resources. Related to this are those resources convertible into a more flexible resource, such as money, or bartered for other resources. Examples include space, equipment, relationships, and expertise.

The point in providing these categories is to have a greater awareness of the substantial amount of actual and potential resources at the disposal of the typical department or program. Another is to be aware of how resources tend to be viewed, that is, into what subconscious categories the variety of resources are sorted.

## Resource Awareness

Intrapreneurship and pervasive leadership are about taking action to improve organizational process and outcomes. However, without resources to invest in new ideas and activities, efforts to bring them to fruition often wither and die. What usually comes first to mind in a discussion of resources is money; however, resource awareness is about seeing the world differently. It is about recognizing the pervasive role of resources in the ability to do our jobs and the existence of resources upon which we draw. So although a dollar figure can probably be placed on most resources, money is not the only resource, and although money is an important and flexible resource, resource enhancement and attraction is not just about raising money. Time, space, equipment, and personnel also are vital resources. The mindset needed is one of seeing the context of work through the lens of resource awareness. An office is not just an office, but a resource. Programming space is a resource. The time spent planning, implementing, and evaluating a program is a resource. The people with whom we work are resources. Beyond the traditional resources of money, time, people, and so forth are the less traditionally considered resources such as information, relationships, expertise, and experience. In the movie *The Matrix*, the ultimate and liberating discovery made by Neo, the hero, is that everything is energy—everything he sees, touches, and uses is energy. Once he discovered this, he was able to shape and use the energy to his advantage. The expectation is readers will realize a parallel discovery—everything is resource. This allows one to shape and use more of the resources in and beyond one's environment to enhance one's practice. Outcomes require both processes and resources, and the resources needed are both traditional and nontraditional.

## Specific Resources

The perspectives of the new science encourage a view beyond traditional resources to the less tangible resources existing within the institution, such as creativity, energy, and commitment. The list of specifics begins with the traditional resources of money, time, people, space, equipment, supplies, basic services, materials, and physical plant, which can be viewed in different, interconnected ways. The commonalities among the traditional resources is their objective, measurable, disconnected nature as experienced in organizations, even the social construction of money and the incorporeal notion of time. Dollars are perceived as real and distinct, as are hours and minutes. This list is followed by the less traditional resources of information, relationships, intrapersonal resources, expertise, experience, and interests and hobbies. Not only are these less tangible and less traditional, but they more clearly reflect some of the aspects of the new paradigm such as context, perspective, patterns, networks, webs, interdependence, complexity, and critical connections.

### Money

Money is the most obvious and apparent of resources, despite the fact that it is a social construction. Even dollar bills in actuality represent a promise, rather than a reality. However, all money is not the same. Money varies in terms of accessibility and restrictions and comes in the form of operating budgets (officially nonrenewable nonsavable, that is, money cannot be saved beyond the current fiscal year, and there is no guarantee as to how much will be received in the next year), rollover accounts (renewable, this is money that is carried over to the following fiscal year), capital budgets (renewable, though typically less flexible than other accounts due to restrictions on how it is to be spent), endowments (renewable), and one's own personal funds (renewable).

## Time

Time is the most ethereal of resources. Despite the pervasiveness of workshops on how to manage, spend, and save time, the notion that time is a renewable or savable resource must be discarded. Such a concept of time is a result of the Newtonian paradigm, which is based on quantification, control, and seeing time as discrete units, rather than as continuous. Money can be banked and accrue interest. Money can be stashed under a mattress and saved for a rainy day. Time, on the other hand, cannot be banked, stashed, or saved. It is a nonrenewable nonsavable resource. It is used well, used poorly, or unused—anyway it is gone. Certainly, better choices about how time is "spent" can be made; however, learning to use time more wisely often only occurs after ridding oneself of notions implying that time is somehow renewable or savable.

## People

A quick search of the Internet on the phrase "people are our greatest resource" revealed two interesting findings. The first is the great variety of corporations, institutions, and organizations making this claim, including Dupont, Sony, the State University of New York at Brockport, the University of Wyoming's Department of Geology and Geophysics, MeriStar Hotels & Resorts, Alliant Energy Corporation, and the United States Air Force. The second is that the word most often preceding this phrase is "our" as in "our people are our greatest resource." The people seen as resources for a student affairs division then would be the professional, clerical, administrative, and paraprofessional staff who work in the division. This is certainly true, but such a narrow view blinds an organization to other people resources, including other students, alumni, volunteers, parents, donors, faculty, staff outside the organizational unit, and community members and leaders. People (relationships are addressed below) are a renewable resource with the potential to generate additional resources.

## Space

Another of the traditionally considered resources, space includes office space, programming space, storage space, work space, and lounge space. When associated with time, space is a nonrenewable nonsavable resource. This may appear counterintuitive because, unlike time, space merely sits there. It can be "saved." However, a different image emerges when one considers hotels, whose business is predicated on the use of space. Hotels cannot stockpile unrented rooms for a period of high demand. Every night that passes without a boarder is revenue gone forever. If space is seen from the perspective of the hotel manager, potential resource generators can be seen, as well as lost revenues through the nonuse of space.

Money in the bank stays there until it is withdrawn and used. While in the bank it is earning interest—it is working. The reality is, however, that money can only be spent once. Space is a resource that can be used over and over again. Resource awareness encourages the view of such nonuse as a failure to capitalize on a resource. While sitting empty it is not generating interest or accruing in value. There may be ways to maximize that resource, or make it work to generate additional resources. For example, depending on the money used to build it (that is, tax-exempt bonds may not allow certain outside groups), a room not being used during the day could be rented to outside groups, thus generating money. Use of a room could be exchanged (bartered) with some group for some other nonmonetary resource they have. Universities' summer conference and housing operations are based on the notion that space can be used to generate resources for other priorities within a division of student affairs.

## Equipment

This category includes office "staples" such as copiers, fax machines, computers, telephones, printers, scanners, and microwaves. Slightly different, but also included in this category is furniture, including such items as desks, tables, chairs, couches, file cabinets, and bookcases. These tend to be nonrenewable because they depreciate and eventually need to be replaced. Some of the depreciation is due to physical wear, some is due to technological obsolescence, and in the case of some furniture, some depreciation is due to changing styles.

## Supplies

This category is the material sitting on the shelves in the supply closet, including paper, tape, ink, disks, pens, pencils, markers, and envelopes. Supplies are typically a nonrenewable savable resource; most wait on the shelf until used.

## Basic Services

Basic services include services such as postage, express mail, local telephone, and long distance telephone. Often a part of operating budgets, these basic services are often taken for granted and are nonrenewable resources.

## Materials

This form of resource goes beyond the notion of supplies and includes items containing data or information use by a program or department, including books, reports, training materials, and journals. Materials are a renewable resource because they can be used again and again, although depreciation occurs owing to going out of date.

## Physical Plant

This category is closely related to space and includes buildings, grounds, lakes, athletic fields, storage facilities, and parking lots. Like space, the physical plant is best seen as a nonrenewable nonsavable resource that can be resource generating. An example of using one's physical plant to generate resources is Wagner College on Staten Island, which rented out its campus for the short-lived television series *Max Bickford*.

## Information

Information is the most basic and most important resource in any organization, because it is what fosters action, development, and innovation in organizations. So although money, time, and space are important resources, information drives the action in organizations. And unlike some of the traditional resources described above, there is no shortage of information. Information is a renewable resource because it can be grown through sharing. When information is shared it multiplies because both the giver and receiver(s) have the information. Information sharing requires freedom of communication. Although totalitarian regimes control money and other physical resources, they most effectively control their population by controlling information.

## Interpersonal Resources

Relationships are closely linked to information because much information is disbursed throughout an organization via relationships. Effective professionals recognize the importance of networking—the building of an informal system of genuine relationships with people who have common concerns and interests and who are willing to assist one another. Relationships link individuals within units, link the units of an organization to each other, and link the organization to its stakeholders and the environmental, social, economic, and political contexts within which it exists. Relationships are a renewable resource and are resource generating, because they generate information and serve as links to other resources. As is described below, relationships are important in resource enhancement and attraction. Student affairs fund-raising (Jackson, 2000; Penney & Rose, 2001) depends on allies, partnerships, teamwork, contacts, champions, stewards, friends-friendships, and associates, all of which are forms of relationships. Relationships have been discussed throughout the book, but to see them as resources truly does challenge student affairs professionals to think differently about their potential.

## Intrapersonal Resources

Relationships are resources that exist through linking individuals, groups, and organizations. Intrapersonal resources are those resources existing within an individual and are both the individual's basic orientation to work and the resources most often drawn upon in times of stress, turmoil, or crisis. Intrapersonal resources are the conscious and subconscious beliefs, attitudes, and tendencies driving a person's behavior. They are affective states, and are different from expertise or skills. They are separated out because they represent a form of affective resource that is often ignored or taken for granted. The list of possible intrapersonal resources is long and includes positive attitude, energy, enthusiasm, initiative, follow-through, self-esteem, dedication, loyalty, commitment, creativity, and a sense of humor. Everyone in an organization brings a host of intrapersonal resources to their work. These are not often considered forms of resources, yet the impact of a lack of energy, enthusiasm, or loyalty is quickly apparent in the performance of any organization. Intrapersonal resources are renewable, especially considering that rest, relaxation, meditation, and retreats are used to *renew* attitudes, enthusiasm, and energy.

## Expertise of Staff

Expertise is another resource category in which the types of expertise brought to bear on one's work and the work of the organization are virtually endless. In addition to the expertise related to a specific job, people often have other types of expertise not listed in a job description that could be brought to bear on their work. Being aware of the broader set of skills held by organizational members makes it more likely that they can be called upon when situations warrant. Expertise and skills include advising, counseling, teaching, technology skills, presenting, group facilitation, topic specific expertise, speaking or writing a foreign language, inter- and intraorganizational understanding, inter- and multicultural competence, training, marketing, promotion, publishing, and grant writing. Expertise is a renewable resource.

### Experience

Experience relates to the number of years people have been in their jobs or at the institution, and their previous job experience. Experience is often not viewed as a resource but, in fact, may be viewed as a detriment to the organization. Organizations seek "new blood" because some longtime staff sometimes are viewed as set in their ways, not open to new ideas, and unable to generate new ideas on their own. Although on the surface and in certain situations this may be the case, it is more likely that the culture of an organization discourages staff from being creative and generating new and exciting ideas. Age and experience are unrelated to one's ability to innovate. One need only think of such famous inventors and innovators as Benjamin Franklin and Leonardo DaVinci as examples of individuals who continued their creative lives well into old age. Experience is a renewable resource.

### Interests and Hobbies

The notion that interests and hobbies are a resource is unusual. More than any of the previous items on this list, this often is considered crossing the line from public (what I do for my job) to private (what I do outside my job). The professional-personal divide is a false dichotomy that is an either-or situation. Instead, it should be seen as another example of both-and. What a person does beyond the job can have an impact on her or his job performance. One need only look at the negative examples of individuals who lost jobs because of something done in their private life. On the positive side there are many examples of persons turning a hobby or an avocation into a life's work. One only needs to be reminded that the entire world-changing industry of personal computers began as personal "hobbies." One's public and private selves overlap and both are brought to the job. So rather than trying to discover how to separate two indivisible sides, organizational members should discuss how to appropriately address the issue. For example, how can someone applying a hobby or interest to their work be compensated or recognized in some way for bringing this gift to bear on the work of the organization?

A list of interests and hobbies would be endless. It is unpredictable how a particular interest or hobby might come into play in the work of an organization. The more interests and hobbies existing in the aggregate in an organization, the greater the amount of diverse information available and probably the more diverse set of relationships individuals in the organization have with people beyond the organization. Interests and hobbies are a renewable resource.

Each of the items and examples in this list is a source of supply, support, or aid used or that could be used to accomplish the work of the organization or invested in new initiatives. An example of a failure to have the mindset of resource awareness is the program director who hired a translator to assist with a visitor from South America who spoke only Spanish. What he did not consider was that one of his clerical staff members spoke Spanish fluently. Financial resources were used where they were not needed instead of going to some other project.

It can be argued as to which resources are renewable or not, or savable or not. However, it is clear the most renewable resources tend to be among the least tangible and the least likely to be included in inventories of departmental resources. As traditional resources (for example, space, physical plant, time, equipment) come to be perceived as nonrenewable and nonsavable, the more likely they will be utilized for resource generation.

The boundaries among the concepts of awareness, enhancement, and attraction are arbitrary because, for instance, resource enhancement begins with the process of increasing resource awareness. Time and energy must be invested in the process of resource awareness, enhancement, and attraction. Obviously, one can see that the time spent in staff selection, training, and development is an investment that pays dividends in the future. Likewise, time and energy need to be invested more directly in resource awareness, enhancement, and attraction activities with the expectation that this will result in better use of existing resources and create additional resources. Such an investment includes identifying the resources in and available to the department or program area, assessing the use of resources in the department or division, and having resource enhancement and attraction as an aspect of the division's strategic planning process. Before moving onto the steps of resource enhancement and resource attraction, the vast array of resources existing in an organization need to be assessed and analyzed. The assessment should

- Inventory the readily quantifiable resources (for example, money, space, equipment, buildings and grounds)

- Create methods for inventorying the less tangible resources (for example, information, relationships, intrapersonal resources)

- Discover and describe how resources are currently being used

- Determine the relative effectiveness and efficiency of resource use as a way to indicate areas needing attention

- Identify the culture (that is, shared values and beliefs) in the organization related to resource enhancement and attraction

- Identify obstacles (for examples, structural obstacles, history and tradition, individual mindsets, policies) to improving the use of those resources

- Create a plan of action related to resource enhancement and attraction

## Resource Enhancement

Resource enhancement is defined as activities focused on renewing, growing, and converting current resources. It is also about maximizing and making most effective use of available resources. Resource enhancement begins with promulgating a resource awareness mindset throughout the organization. It also involves assessing and analyzing the current use of organizational resources, seeking ways to convert nonrenewable and nonsavable resources, renewing and growing the less tangible resources identified in the previous section, and shifting resources where appropriate to maximize their impact on the work of the organization.

### Converting Resources

Converting resources is the process of taking resources, especially those that are nonrenewable nonsavable, and using them to generate more flexible resources (for example, money, expertise, information). Identifying the nonrenewable nonsavable resources may not be easy, because these types of resources are often mistaken for savable resources. Nonrenewable nonsavable resources may include space, physical plant, and equipment. Other convertible resources include materials, information, and expertise. Simple examples of converting resources already mentioned include identifying spaces that can be rented or bartered to some other group or organization, renting out parts of the campus to outside organizations, and creating a conference program to use campus spaces during down times. Other examples of converting resources include trading materials, information, or expertise with other departments or programs. For example, rather than hiring someone to provide training for the organization, organizations could be identified with which particular training expertise could be "traded." Again, this form of barter may save monetary resources that could be used to address other organizational needs.

**Growing Resources**

Although it is possible to grow virtually any resource, some growth requires the investment of money, such as adding space or staff. The focus of this section is on resources not requiring money to grow. These include the less tangible resources of relationships, information, intrapersonal resources, expertise, and experience. Because of the importance of relationships, they are discussed in a separate section (Growing Relationships). As indicated above, less tangible resources need to be inventoried. Individuals and groups within the organization also need to adopt a mindset of intentionality and strategy when it comes to the intangible resources of an organization. Too often the development and use of resources such as relationships, information, and expertise are left to happenstance and idiosyncrasy.

*Information*

Information is the lifeblood of an organization. The best way to destroy a person's ability to perform her or his job is to cut them off from the information necessary for them to do the job. However, professionals do not often suffer from a shortage of information and, in fact, may be overwhelmed by the amount of information received. This burgeoning mass of information is why companies specializing in information management and information technology continue to grow and develop. Organizations need help to manage the information already coursing through their systems. So "growing" information is probably not the precise verb to use with regard to this resource. What does need to grow is the effective management of information and the ability to guide and direct the collection, access, and use of information to effectively manage the overall organizations.

One area of administrative information about which there are often questionable cultural assumptions and accessibility issues is the budget, the document specifying the use and distribution of monetary resources for the organizational unit. Departmental and programmatic budgets contain a great deal of information, yet in many organizations the process of budget development and the budget itself are shrouded in secrecy. When information is viewed as a vital resource and the budget is recognized as a vital source of information, the assumptions about who should have access to this information can be called into question.

### Intrapersonal Resources

The goal in growing intrapersonal resources is to maximize the positive beliefs, attitudes, and tendencies in individuals throughout the organization. A first step is investing time in discovering both the areas of positive intrapersonal resources and any pockets of negative attitudes and beliefs that drain or negate the positive attitudes and beliefs in the organization. This involves a process of self-discovery and self-awareness on the part of individuals, and such an exercise requires a climate of trust, honesty, and mutual respect. On an individual level, the process can involve a retreat or retreat-like activities to facilitate self-discovery. On the organizational level, given the relationship of individual attitudes to shared beliefs of an organization's culture, conducting a cultural audit would help discover any negative shared beliefs or attitudes reinforced by the organization's culture and find ways to change those beliefs and attitudes.

### Expertise

Expertise is an area in which the culture and policies in many organizations encourage the professional development of staff. Such development is most often directed by the interests and perceived needs of the individual staff member. However, in addition to self-directed professional development, organizations also should intentionally and strategically identify areas of expertise needed for the effective functioning and continued growth of the organization. Organizational resources can then be used to encourage staff members to focus their development activities on those particular areas.

*Experience*

One might assume that the only way to grow experience is to wait and time will take care of it. Unfortunately, that is not the case, especially in American culture where ideas of experience and wisdom are not considered as important as today's newest idea. Therefore, to "grow" experience, the shared cultural beliefs regarding longtime members and the beliefs of those longtime members of an organization need to be considered. For example, is it taken for granted that anyone who has been with the organization for a long time no longer has anything vital to contribute to the future of the organization? Are long-term employees assumed to be obstacles to change? These beliefs need to be examined and either dismantled when found to be false or addressed if found to be valid. The taken-for-granted beliefs of longtime members also need to be examined. Have they come to internalize the assumption that their perspectives and experiences are not welcome in discussions of the organization's future? Have they ceased to generate new ideas, because others assume that they do not possess the ability to come up with new ideas? Again, these beliefs need to be examined and any negative beliefs (either of the individuals or of the organization) need to be addressed.

## Growing Relationships

As the key determinants of any action and processes in organizations, relationships are central to most resource enhancement and attraction strategies, especially fund raising. Partnering is an important resource skill and is built on mutual trust, mutual need, a willingness to help one another, a commitment to generate results bigger than the individual parties themselves, and a commitment to the future (Sturtevant, 1997). Partnering is not solely self-serving. There is also mutuality and commitment to the individuals and organizations with whom someone partners. Yet only when an individual is in relationship with other individuals, programs, and departments can someone become aware of their partner's needs and how those needs relate to one's own.

The link between relationships and fund-raising is evident. A prime example of this phenomenon is the many organizations, including universities and colleges, who are shifting their terminology from fund-raising to friend-raising. The organization, while interested in receiving funds, recognizes that it wants involvement on the part of the individual. Friends typically have some kind of mutual interest or shared values. The organization extends its sphere of support and influence. These "friends" now have a stake in the success of the venture. Friend-raising tends to enhance and attract more resources than merely fund-raising. So a benefit of friend-raising is that it often involves obtaining diverse resources, including information, contacts, connections, and expertise, as well as monetary donations.

As with other resources, before one can focus on growth, the relationships of the individuals and groups in the organization must be inventoried. This involves identifying with whom people have relationships in other programs, departments, and divisions in the institution and with which individuals and groups beyond the institution. It also involves ascertaining the type (for example, acquaintance, friend, colleague, now working together, have worked together) and intensity (for example, see at conferences, in regular contact, there when needed) of the relationship. The number of relationships in an organization of even moderate size is enormous, so an initial inventory may be for staff members to identify the ten to fifteen relationships in the organization and ten outside the organization contributing most to their work. Most student affairs professionals have connections with a vast number of people in the field. They will have similar numbers of connections with people outside of the field. The results of such an inventory are often eye-opening and provide a picture of an interlinked network of valuable resources. Conducting an inventory is a form of growth because it makes available to the entire organization many of the relationships formerly restricted to an individual or a small group of people. Like information, sharing relationships within the organization multiplies the relationships.

Once relationships have been inventoried, it is then possible to discuss and strategize with which individuals and organizations relationships are to be sought. This might take the form of building on a relationship that an individual staff member has with a person or group, or it could involve identifying individuals and groups important to the work of the organization but with whom no one in the organization currently has a relationship.

The specific relationships important to an organization will vary. However, there are particular relationships that need to be created. It is vital that relationships be built between the student affairs division and the institutional advancement and development unit. This can take the form of assigning a representative from student affairs to that office to act as a liaison. Other resource-related departments with whom there should be active relationships include alumni affairs, public relations, marketing, university relations, and governmental affairs.

### Shifting Resources

The notion of shifting resources recognizes that student affairs divisions can expect little if any budgetary growth in the near term. Attracting new resources is important and is addressed in the next section. Shifting resources is a form of growth through substitution. Jones (1993) pointed out that most budget processes focus primarily on the base or continuation budget and fail to incorporate an investment strategy, that is, identify current dollars available to fund new initiative and innovations. Breneman and Taylor (1996) indicated that colleges and universities are beginning to take the advice of policy analysts and practice growth by substitution, which means for every new activity initiated, an old one must be discontinued. This process requires that enhancements and initiatives be funded by savings in the budget, rather than by additions to the budget.

Strategic, as opposed to incremental, reallocation of budgets is typically a more effective use of resources (Jones, 1993). An important
aspect of strategic resource reallocation is that it can promote
intrapreneurial activity. It is not just money that is needed for the
development of initiatives, but time as well. Therefore, organizations need to create ways to pool time and provide time in the form
of grants for pursuit of good ideas. For the individuals involved, this
should result in a reduction of other responsibilities.

### Sharing Resources

Resource sharing is a form of resource enhancement because in the
sharing a savings is made, and the resources saved can be invested
in other organizational activities. Sharing at the program or department level can include sharing equipment (for example, copier, fax
machine, microwave), space, personnel, technology, and materials.

## Resource Attraction

Resource attraction is the process of bringing new resources into a
program, division, or institution. In fact, the most significant area
of administrative growth and focus in higher education during the
past several decades is in the area of institutional advancement and
development (Gordon, Strode, & Brady, 1993). The resource constraints plaguing higher education during the past several decades
led to a trend in which virtually all institutions, including public
four-year colleges and community colleges, are now fund-raising and
instituting capital campaigns (Brambach & Bumphus, 1993; Miser
& Mathias, 1993; Nicklin, 1992). Many larger student affairs divisions are hiring development professionals. This is a positive development; however, there is a danger as well. As with other situations
in which a specialist is brought into a program, the others in the
organization often feel less obliged to address the issue. Professionals become further sequestered in their individual silos. A case in
point is the faculty person of color hired into a department where

all the other faculty are white. These individuals are often inundated with the needs of all the students of color, because the students may prefer to speak to a person of color, but also because white faculty no longer see the needs of students of color as their concern. This dynamic needs to be addressed and avoided in the area of resource attraction. It is not that everyone should be on the phone tracking down potential donors, but all organizational members need to view their world through the lens of resource awareness, enhancement, and attraction, a view that will then be of assistance to the development officer and to the division overall. Professionals are both hall directors and resource attractors, academic advisors and resource attractors, and deans and resource attractors. Student affairs divisions also need to overcome the assumption on the part of the institution's leadership that student affairs is not viable as a fundraising sector within the institution (Shay, 1993). Any resource attraction activities conducted by the division of student affairs and its members must be done in coordination with institutional resource attraction activities, and specifically with the institution's development office. It is inappropriate, ineffective, and politically dangerous to have conflicts emerge or mixed messages sent due to a lack of communication between the student affairs division and the development office. Resource attraction is often linked with and supports intrapreneurial activities and takes on several forms, including fundraising, grant writing, and partnerships.

### Fundraising

Fundraising refers to the solicitation of funds and gifts from alumni and alumnae, internal and external constituents and stakeholders, community members, and public and private foundations. The purpose of fundraising is to help institutions and their organizational units meet their goals and enhance their ability to serve the needs of constituents and stakeholders (Brambach & Bumphus, 1993). From 1966 to 1996, there was an almost tenfold increase in dollar support to higher education through fund-raising efforts (Council for Aid to Education, 1996). The total contributions to higher education from all sources reached an estimated 14.25 billion dollars in the 1995–1996 academic year. So although the total number of dollars may have declined during the economic downturn at the beginning of this century, there are still plenty of dollars being contributed to higher education and it is necessary for student affairs staff to increase their role in fundraising.

Many of the skills and characteristics of a successful fundraiser are the same as those of the successful student affairs professional (Penney & Rose, 2001), including being self-motivated, dedicated, interested in students, able to work alone, cognizant of staff and student needs, and willing to try new ways of practicing, as well as being a planner, risk taker, and an effective verbal and written communicator. Jackson (2000) points out that training is often available through the development office for student affairs staff interested in working on fund-raising efforts. Given that many student affairs professionals already reflect the characteristics of fundraisers, such training will be more effective in creating the skill and knowledge base for successfully adding the role of fundraiser to one's experience base.

Student affairs divisions need to link planning with fundraising efforts, and the priorities of the division with private donor goals (Iannozzi, 2002). Private donors often want their money to go toward something specific and have may strategic plans of their own. Student affairs divisions must find ways to work these donors' perspectives into their own planning and budgeting strategies. This does not mean divisions of student affairs should shift their priorities to match a donor. Instead, they need to discover donors whose priorities already match their own and donors whose priorities could match theirs if the donor's priorities were redefined in some way. The intention of the donor may remain the same; however, how that intention is brought into reality could be in a way they had not considered.

Although not meant to be an exhaustive description of fund-raising issues and practices, the rest of this section reviews the basic skills of successful fund-raisers, reasons people donate, the types and potential targets of fund-raising, and the notion of stewardship.

## Basic Skills of Successful Fundraisers

In addition to arguing that successful student affairs professionals and successful fundraisers look a lot alike, Penney and Rose (2001) identified the basic skills of successful fundraisers:

- A desire to succeed

- Communication skills (verbal, written, and active listening)

- Partnering skills (that is, relationship building)

- A willingness to "make the ask" (that is, actually asking a potential donor for a donation)

- Perseverance, persistence, and a tolerance for delayed gratification

The one ability that stands out as perhaps not yet in most student affairs professionals' skill set is the willingness to "make the ask." This is a difficult step for most neophyte fund-raisers or people for whom fundraising is not their primary job responsibility. It conjures up images and feelings about neediness, powerlessness, and inadequacy, and it can cause embarrassment. However, although a great deal of effort goes into the cultivation of a donor, "making the ask" is *the* crucial step of fundraising. The money does not come unless someone asks for it.

## Understanding Why People Donate

There are many reasons that individuals donate money to a particular organization. Warwick (2001) identified twenty-three reasons people choose to donate. Those related to student affairs fund-raising are

> Because they are asked
>
> They support organizations similar to student affairs
>
> They believe the gift will make a difference
>
> They are recognized for their donation
>
> It enables them to do something about a critical issue
>
> Because of the connections and relationships such a donation may engender
>
> It gives them the sense of belonging to something greater
>
> It helps them preserve their worldview by validating cherished values and beliefs
>
> It gives them tax benefits
>
> They feel it is their duty

It is also important to realize that an appeal will trigger a gift if it brings to life the feelings that move people to act. Student affairs programs and initiatives address many critical issues of interest to potential donors (for example, alcohol and drug issues, violence, access, persistence). Such issues should be targeted for fundraising efforts.

### Types and Targets of Fundraising

Types of fundraising that can be directed at the divisional level (and coordinated with the development office) include annual giving programs (focusing on trustees involved with the work of the division, students, alumni, and parents), personal solicitations, direct-mail solicitation, phone-a-thons, corporate and foundation support, and small business solicitation (Breneman & Taylor, 1996). The types of programs that would be good targets for donor support include student leadership programs, student scholarships, diversity and multicultural programs, health promotion programs, internship and mentoring programs, and community and volunteer service programs (Jackson, 2000).

Some smaller potential donors, especially younger alumni and alumnae, are less likely to give because they believe their gift is not large enough to make a difference and because they believe they just gave through tuition and fees (Pulley, 2000). These smaller donors and younger alumni and alumnae, who will eventually have more money to give, should be targets for student affairs. Student affairs staff can convince people that there is a good reason to give money to a particular program, and that something important and interesting will be done with their gift, no matter how small. Sometimes inviting potential donors onto campus, into the residence halls, or to programming events can help them see the difference their gift could make. This is good rationale for student affairs staff to focus on smaller gifts (while not ignoring larger gifts, of course). In addition to financial donations, new donors may also be interested in contributing their expertise. This is an avenue for possible partnerships and a source of expertise perhaps not in evidence in the current organization.

*Stewardship*

Stewardship represents a special relationship in which there is a long-term commitment made to the donor. It reinforces the importance of relationships in the fundraising process. Once an individual commits resources to the organization it becomes the professional obligation of those accepting the donation to follow through on that commitment. This includes expressing immediate appreciation from the organization and the individuals with whom the donors worked, keeping in touch with the donor about the program or activity to which they donated, providing more formal recognition, and inviting that individual to take part in organizational activities where appropriate.

## Grant Writing

Grant writing is a particular type of fundraising, and distinct enough to warrant its own focus. Like the object of fundraising, a grant is an award of money or other resources or both, but is from a private foundation or public or governmental agency and typically for a specific purpose. Foundations are nonprofit organizations whose purpose is to distribute resources to individuals and groups according to their specific mission. There are several types of foundations. For example, independent foundations are funded through individual or family gifts, community foundations are established to benefit community projects and organizations, and corporate foundations are established by business organizations to address community needs.

Grants can be obtained for a variety of purposes but typically are sought for research projects or program development or enhancement. The purpose of the research or program must align with the goals and mission of the granting agency. What is most important for student affairs professionals to realize is that there is money available to fund innovative projects and programs. Currently, there are more than 50,000 private foundations in the United States (Foundation Center, n.d.). This compares to 22,000 private foundations in 1980. In fact, from 1997 to 1999, 5,200 new grant makers came into being. Despite the economic downturn and reduced giving by foundations, higher education continues to receive the largest share of that funding, about a quarter of all grant dollars distributed.

Virtually every university and most colleges have an office to assist individuals in identifying appropriate funding sources, crafting a grant proposal, and administering funded projects. Even if an institution does not have such an office, assistance in obtaining grants is available in the form of a host of publications about grant writing and through Web sites such as foundationcenter.com. Although writing skills are important in the grant writing process, what is more important is the initiative to pursue a grant to support a project or program, the idea itself, and knowledge of the grant writing and funding process. Taking advantage of competitive awards means knowing how to craft a grant proposal to meet the specifications of the chosen granting agency. A grant proposal is written to effectively articulate what the idea is, how it is designed to meet organization goals and objectives, and how the idea also meets the foundation's mission. Although it is important to know the typical components of a grant (for example, abstract, project description, budget, dissemination plans), organizing one's thoughts before the actual writing of the grant is critical. A proposal can be built around several basic questions, such as, Who is the organization? What is the project and its objectives? How will the goals of the project be achieved? How much will the project cost? Why and how much external funding is needed? When will the project be completed? If successful, how will the results of this project be shared with other institutions (that is, dissemination plans)?

### Partnerships

Partnerships are another way to bring new resources into an organization. Partnerships are structured relationships that take many forms, including interdivisional, interinstitutional, and business or corporate partnerships. Any partnership requires some common mission, purpose, or activity among partners. Beder (1984) identified four other key components in the development of partnerships. The first is the degree of reciprocity between partners, that is, the balance between giving and receiving resources. The second is system openness, the degree to which the organization is receptive to relationships with external parties. Another component is trust and commitment, described as the interdependence between the partners as well as how committed both sides are to the partnership. The final component is the degree to which structures are fluid and flexible to allow for adaptability during the course of the partnership. Collaborative partnerships allow student affairs professionals to develop intrapreneurial skills by working with external constituencies to gain resources in support of internal initiatives. Such partnerships can include area businesses in the construction or redesign of residence halls to accommodate business conferences during the summer, or designing computer labs also to be used by businesses to develop their workforce. Although partnerships may be a way to increase resources or access to resources, they also may be a way to save money and, therefore, make it possible to direct existing funds to other needed areas—a form of resource shifting.

*Interdivisional*

Interdivisional partnerships are those existing within the institution but across separate divisions. A prime example is partnerships between student affairs and academic affairs. Such a partnership could involve linking faculty research interests with student affairs programs to enhance attractiveness to funding agencies. For example, many institutions implement programs to address alcohol and drug problems or violence problems. There may be faculty in sociology or health studies who have one of these areas as a research focus. A partnership could result in a much stronger and theoretically grounded proposal lending itself to a high-quality evaluation and a research component. Examples of other academic and student affairs partnerships include residential living-learning centers, learning communities, and community service and service learning initiatives. Depending on the configuration of the institution's organizational structure, other potential partners include institutional advancement and development, and enrollment management.

*Interinstitutional*

Interinstitutional partnerships are university-to-university partnerships, and have been labeled as consortia, cooperative planning, collaborative arrangements, and intercollegiate cooperation. In an era of constrained resources, it makes sense for institutions to work together to reduce the competition that serves to drain both institutions. In this sense, interinstitutional partnerships are a form of resource sharing whereby two or more institutions come together to provide new programs and services or combine current programs and services (Tushnet, 1993). Examples of this form of partnership are the library relationships among institutions, cooperative course offerings, student and faculty exchange programs, combined professional and faculty training and development, shared facilities, shared technological support, inter-institutional research and planning, and collaborative student recruitment and admissions. Other shared services have included counseling, health services, activities programming, career counseling, and academic advising. Shared management is another form of partnership and involves functions such as physical plant maintenance, health services, transportation, and security. It appears that shared services and shared management functions are very straightforward forms of partnership for geographically proximate institutions. Of course, proximity becomes less of an issue with the Internet. The toughest obstacles to partnering with other institutions are the assumptions within individual professionals, and perhaps the greatest obstacles to university partnerships are the perceived need for competition among institutions and the fear of losing institutional identity through collaboration (Woodard et al., 2000).

### Corporate, Business, Industry

Partnerships between businesses and student affairs divisions are a viable, necessary, and emerging form of resource attraction. Such partnerships are a standard practice in community colleges, where vocational education, management training, and workforce development have matched business and community needs with institutional expertise. Such partnerships are also growing among universities; however, it is an area in which student affairs has lagged behind. A business partnership is a relationship between institutions or individual programs and businesses that is characterized by mutual cooperation and responsibility, typically for the achievement of a specific goal. A partnership is not merely soliciting local businesses for funds, outsourcing, or contracting for services. Instead, it is working together to achieve a common end. Partnerships yield much needed resources in many forms for institutions, including innovative ideas, new technology, monetary returns, service in kind, advisory services, and student placements (Utah Partners in Education, n.d.). One of the largest advantages of a business-university partnership is the potential to integrate working and learning experiences for students through internships, co-ops, and job placement.

———————

Resources are the lifeblood of any organization. They make work, innovation, and outcomes possible. The more one is able to perceive and be aware of the resources that course through the organization, the more one can bring intentionality to bear on the use of resources, see potential improvements in current functions, and see new ideas and new initiatives as possible. The notion of "everything as resource" can serve to increase the motivation, creativity, innovation, and morale (forms of intrapersonal resources!) of the members of the organization. Once "everything as resource" is adopted it becomes easier to see how current resources can be enhanced and how to attract additional resources to the organization. This complex view of resources is applied to the specific resource of technology in the next chapter.

# 6

# Technology as Brush, Paint, and Artist

The previous chapter addressed the pervasiveness of resources in student affairs work. The one resource that is rapidly and totally permeating student affairs work is technology. There is hardly a sector of student affairs that has not had to adjust to or incorporate advanced technology during the past decade. As described throughout this chapter, technology and its role in our work address each of the four elements of the conceptual framework underlying the arguments in this book: valuing dualisms, transcending paradigms, recognizing connections, and embracing paradox. Yet perhaps the most salient point about technology is represented by the fact that this is a chapter about technology in a book written by two people with the most basic of technological know-how. Our combined knowledge of technology and technological innovations in higher education can be accurately portrayed as minimal. Yet we are writing about technology. That is the point! Technology cannot be left to the techies. An important competency needed for effective student affairs practice now and in the future is a technology mindset—the willingness to perceive, critically engage with, adapt, apply, and assess technology in student affairs work.

Using and understanding technology are two different things. A person can understand how to use technological resources without understanding how to actually program a Web site. This chapter focuses on transcendent issues related to technology, not on the how-to's of software or hardware. The title of this chapter, "Technology as Brush, Paint, and Artist," focuses on the argument that technology is

- A tool to assist in work (brush)

- A medium shaped by professionals through which work is accomplished (paint)

- The technological skills and mindset of the individual professional brought to bear on the problems and issues in student affairs work (artist)

Technology is viewed through a wide-lens perspective as opposed to a microscopic lens that focuses on the details of technological adaptations, because technology and its application to the various dimensions of student affairs work is evolving so rapidly as to make any discussion of software or hardware meaningless. Even language is evolving at a more rapid pace than print technology can account for. An example of this evolution is that throughout the decade of the 1990s, Kent State University's master's program in college student personnel had a required course entitled, "Microcomputers for Administrators." The name itself became virtually meaningless by the end of the decade—no one talks about microcomputers anymore. The content of the course changed every time it was offered. At the start of the decade course topics included word processing, e-mail, and database management software. By the end of the decade most of the focus was on integrated information systems, Web site development, and distance education modalities. Nothing about the course remained the same after several years. However, the important point was that the course continued to be offered. It was not eliminated once word processing and e-mail became as pervasive as paper, pens, and postage. The existence of the course indicated the priority that the program faculty placed on student affairs professionals to be focused on technology as an important tool for doing their work.

Another reason for taking a broad perspective is captured by Upcraft, Terenzini, and Kruger (1999), who were "disturbed that much of . . . technology is being embraced uncritically, with little or no analysis of its potential consequences, for good or for ill" (p. 30). All student affairs professionals need to be critically engaged with technology. Critical engagement transcends the dichotomies of acceptance or rejection and openness or skepticism. Engagement implies more than knowledge of technological applications; it requires interaction, use, assessment, and observation of the impact of technology on varying aspects of student affairs work. Criticalness is needed at two levels: single-loop and double-loop levels (Argyris & Schön, 1996). Technological applications need to be critically analyzed for what they purport to do. Does the student information system provide the access and ability to analyze student records that are needed? That is a single-loop question. Double-loop criticalness asks, Is this the best way through which records can be managed? What is lost by using this particular system? What unintended consequences to shifting to another technology might emerge? The concern is whereas technology is pervading student affairs, a critically engaged mindset is lacking.

The changes occurring in society are often described as being a result of a *wave* of technology, as though technology washes over people. A wave mindset leaves student affairs professionals at the mercy of whatever changes are dropped upon them. Such disempowerment contradicts the arguments in this book—complexity and chaos cannot be predicted or controlled, but they can be influenced. Critical engagement requires efforts to enhance awareness and a willingness to engage—engage in conversation with technological experts, with the technology itself, with students about the role and uses of technology in their lives, and with assessment of technology and its influence on students, student affairs work, and the ability to reach institutional goals. In order to effectively engage with technology and its implications and applications, one must first enhance one's awareness of technology and its pervasive and evolving influence on one's life, both personally and professionally. Technology needs to be understood as brush, paint, *and* artist.

## Technology as Brush

Technology as brush implies that it is a tool for accomplishing the educational and administrative aspects of student affairs work. Technological developments are often seen as ends in and of themselves. However, when viewed as a tool—as a means, not an end—professionals are more likely to use technology to address the goals and principles of their work. Therefore, individuals must not lose sight of their vision. Professionals must ensure that technology serves educational purposes and does not take away from them. For example, one of the authors had a conversation with a senior technology officer at a university. In describing how he saw his job, this person said: "Do you remember the 'ah-ha' moments you had in college when something clicked for you? It may be when the professor worked out a math problem on the blackboard and for the first time you understood the logic. Or it might have been when something in a discussion in one class made something you learned in another class more meaningful. That's my criteria for technology. Does it increase those 'ah-ha' moments or does it get in the way of them occurring? If it increases the 'ah-ha' moments then we need to have it; if it doesn't, then we don't." Although this example is drawn from classroom pedagogy it is also applicable to student affairs. What drives the action in any organization are the values and principles of the members of that organization. Meeting student needs is among the shared values in student affairs organizations, and certainly meeting student needs is one of the purposes for the technological innovations listed in the previous section. An administrative example is related to personal digital assistants (PDAs, such as a Palm Pilot). Ramapo College of New Jersey provides PDAs to staff that contain housing rosters, banned student lists, protocols, and forms (Chang, 2002). The PDAs replaced the need to print, transport, and consult unwieldy binders for the necessary information. It provided an administrative "ah-ha" moment.

New technology is being created and promulgated every day. At some point in the late 1980s, some residence life person came up with the idea of using beepers and pagers for on-duty professionals rather than having the on-duty staff members remain in their offices or apartments by the telephone. Beepers were not created for this purpose. It took someone coming up with the idea, and convincing her or his supervisor that such a system would enhance the staff's ability to respond to crises. This is an example of viewing technology as a tool but also from a mindset of critical engagement.

Technological tools come with by-products. By-products are unanticipated consequences or outcomes resulting from the use or implementation of a technological process or product. These by-products can be good or bad. They can either contribute in some way to the teaching and learning process or enhance student experiences, or they can detract in some way. Examples of technological by-products can be seen in residence halls. Thirty years ago, many residence halls did not have telephones in student rooms. Students congregated around the hall or building telephone to converse with loved ones or friends. Today, virtually every residence hall room has a telephone, television cable access, and an Internet port. One of the by-products of this change is that to a greater degree today than fifteen or twenty years ago, students are more isolated in their rooms, a trend referred to as "cocooning" (Upcraft, Terenzini, & Kruger, 1999). Community building is a greater challenge for today's residence hall staffs. Now cell phones are threatening to make residence hall telephone systems obsolete and dramatically increase the administrative costs to residence life departments because each time staff members want to call a student on campus who has not activated her or his residence hall phone, they have to dial a long-distance number to reach them on their cell phone! Those who believe in the values of community in the residence halls may describe the above as a negative by-product, but there are examples of positive by-products as well, such as the one cited earlier—Ramapo College's use of PDAs to assist in crisis and emergency response for residence life. Student affairs professionals need to be more conscious and aware of technology as it enters their spheres of influence and thus be in a better position to assess the impact of newly introduced tools on the ability to do their jobs, enact their values and principles, and be sensitive to and on the lookout for by-products of technological applications and advances. Professionals who have an assessment mindset and work in programs or departments seeking to shape their practice through assessment enhance such technological sensitivity.

## Technology as Paint

The image of technology as paint indicates that it is a medium through which work is done. It is not the work itself, neither is it purely a tool, but it profoundly affects the way work is accomplished. For example, e-mail is both a tool and a medium that affects interpersonal communication. The role and influence of technological media in the transformation of higher education and student affairs work is an example of a both-and situation, rather than an either-or. Technology both did and did not transform higher education, and is and is not transforming higher education. It is now tempting to say that the technology revolution of the 1990s fell far short of the promise (some would say threat) to radically alter the higher education landscape. Paralleling the collapse of the dot-com economic revolution at the beginning of this new millennium has been the retrenchment of the initiatives of many institutions in what was supposed to be the next great wave of technological transformation in higher education—distance education. Many distance education spin-offs from universities collapsed or have been quietly folded back into the mainstream parts of campus in the first years of this decade.

In the late 1990s, predictions were made that physical campuses would decline in importance, if not disappear altogether. Although no one can say what will happen twenty years from now, it is clear that students did not flood to these distance education opportunities as anticipated, and traditional college attendance continues to be robust even in the face of the recession experienced at the beginning of this decade. Educators have been reminded yet again that experiencing college, academics, teaching, and learning is not the same online (or on television) as it is in person. Yet the underlying assumption of many of the distance education efforts was that it was. This is similar to the assumption that online publications are the same as hard copy. Universities are loading reams of documents online to save money, and many professional organizations in higher education and student affairs have shifted journals and other publications to an online only format. However, students, faculty, and staff do not read online materials in the same way or to the same degree as hard copy (O'Hara & Sellen, 1997). We have gained a financial savings; however, we have not assessed the loss in readership or in comprehension in the shift to this medium of communication. Beyond that, many people print out the online material, so the economic and environmental savings may not be what was hoped for.

Midcareer or later professionals can recall how various waves of technological innovations were supposed to transform or replace traditional educational practice. Television was one such marvel. In the 1960s and 1970s, it was anticipated that classes would be beamed right into people's living rooms. The best faculty would teach thousands of students at one time. Of course, that revolution did not happen. Other technological innovations with the expectation of transformational power included film, real-time online video, the VCR, videodisks, DVD, and CD-ROM. So it is true that when viewed from the university level, technology did not radically alter higher education.

But it is also true that technology has and is transforming higher education—transforming it from within. Again, this dynamic represents both-and, not either-or. Despite the experience of the relative lack of the radical transformation anticipated in the late 1990s, technology probably more than anything else (including economic downturns) has the power and potential to dramatically reorder the institutional universe in a brief span of time. There has been a vast array of technological innovations and inventions, and they continue to emerge, each having the potential to transform aspects of the higher education experience. Each could be *the* butterfly whose wing flap sets off a cascade of transformations. One need only look at the impact the Internet has had on other industries. One must not be blinded by the collapse of the dot-com revolution to the potential impact of technology. To do so would result in missing the dramatic examples of shifts and changes that have occurred. Take, for example, the travel industry. Prior to the early 1990s, the only way to book an airline flight was through a travel agent or to call an airline directly. Internet access to travel services has caused a tremendous shakeout in the travel industry, which has had to dramatically alter its image and its client base to survive. It is now focusing almost solely on high-end travelers, group travel, and complex itineraries.

Given the proliferation of technological applications, similar transformations may be in the offing for student affairs. For example, Web-based student services at various universities have proliferated and include

- Admissions: a vast array of institutional information available online, online applications, Web-based tours; the Internet is the first place to obtain information about an institution

- Financial aid: online resources, processes, applications

- Orientation: schedules, orientation quizzes and scavenger hunts, evaluation, direct marketing

- Academic advising: online advising, electronic learning, portfolio development

- Student union, student activities: room reservation systems, student group Web pages

- Residence life: housing sign-up, resident advisor applications, photos of students banned from the residence halls, including digital photos with damage and incident reports

- Career center: career information, frequently asked questions (FAQs), online career advising, online employment portfolios

- Registrar: registration, grades, course schedule, transcript review, course and professor evaluations

- Service learning: volunteer and agency or site registration

- Bursar: billing status

- Other: online writing tutors, collegewide phone directories (some downloadable to PDAs)

Although these are primarily administrative functions rather than educational functions, when viewed from the lens of the new science one becomes sensitive to the fact that any one of these changes can have an amplifying effect and cause significant transformative change throughout the system. This is one reason that it is important to realize that technology is neither value neutral nor benign. Just as there are no "neutral" actions, there is no "neutral" technology. Technology has an impact on what professionals do and how they do it. Farson (1996) points out the paradox that people invent technology, and technology invents and shapes people. He provides the example that although humans invented the automobile, it was the automobile that created modern cities and suburbs and, in turn, altered courtship patterns, sexual practices, and the social environment of the humans who created the technology. Today's multinational corporations are only possible because of the advances in telecommunications. Technologies are created to

address problems, needs, and desires; however, there are unanticipated consequences of adopting technological innovations. In fact,
another paradox identified by Farson is that not only do the technologies shape people, but technology often creates the opposite of
its intended purpose. For example, computers and electronic communication were to bring about the paperless office. Instead, there
is dramatically more paper being used. In addition, there are uses
for the technology that go beyond what could have been imagined,
so tasks are often added each time another form of technology is
adopted. So rather than technology helping reduce workload, it
actually adds to it. Student Information Systems (SIS) provides a
prime example. Prior to the adoption of electronic tracking and data
storage, "SIS" consisted of the registrar's staff recording grades, cer-
tifying graduates, and processing dismissals and withdrawals. Of
course, the registrar's staff did more than that, but the point is that
given the technology of paper, pens, and physical file storage, there
was a limit to what staff could be asked to do. Today, with the incorporation of electronic or intranet-based SIS, so much more is
demanded of the registrar. In fact, the entire administrative division of enrollment management could not exist as it has evolved
without the technological advances made in records tracking and
processing. This technology comes with hidden costs. For example,
in addition to the registrar's staff, there is now an expensive cadre
of administrative technology professionals to maintain and upgrade
the system and work with the administrators who use the system to
make it do what they need it to do.

Also on the administrative side of higher education and student
affairs, there has been the hope and dream that technology would
make administrative and management life more efficient and cost
effective. This is a pipe dream. No one has a paperless office. The
expectation that technological innovations and applications will
result in cost reductions must be eliminated. The overwhelming evidence says any cost reduction is an illusion, as costs, in addition to
hardware and software purchases and upgrades, are generally shifted

to other areas (for example, from data entry clerks to network maintenance personnel) and are less visible (for example, the increased need for staff training and retraining). Plus, usually the more information an office has the capacity to collect and store, the more information it collects and stores. Decisions related to technology adoption and application should not be made on potential cost savings, but on the ability to more effectively meet the needs of the organizational unit and, in turn, students.

Technology is a medium to be shaped to the needs and purposes of student affairs work. As technology increases in sophistication, the ability to shape it to specific needs is also increased. Using technology in different ways is one way of shaping it. However, this section focuses on shaping, changing, or improving the technology itself to meet student needs. This involves transcending traditional boundaries, communicating, and partnering with people inside and outside the institution, depending on what kind of shaping is desired. This is part of recognizing connections. The first step in this process is saying, "Gee, I wish my (choose one: cell phone, PDA, laptop, PowerPoint, SIS) could _____ (fill in the blank)." This expresses the desire to shape the technology to meet one's needs. The second step is to contact the company (if the product/process is external) or the technology department (if the product or process is internal) and share the idea. Companies who design and manufacture such products want to hear from end users. Technology companies have research and development units whose purpose is to come up with new ideas and develop new products, but many companies get some of their new ideas from the people who use the product, either formally through company sponsored focus groups or informally through unsolicited feedback. Again, the people providing feedback are not just techies looking for another gizmo, but front–line, not necessarily technologically inclined, people using the product in real life. Given the competition in the technology marketplace, the turnaround for improving an existing product is fairly short, certainly shorter than if someone called Ford with an idea for improving one of their automobiles. Therefore, the person suggesting the idea might actually see it come to market and be able to use it in their job.

## Technology as Artist

The image of technology as artist serves as a reminder that technology has a human dimension as well. It encompasses the technological skills and mindsets brought to bear on the problems and issues in student affairs work. A professional's attitude toward technology influences his or her willingness and ability to critically engage with technology. Attitudes about technology are related to attitudes about change and innovation.

At one end of the change-technology continuum are those who seek out the next technological innovation and try to figure out how it can be incorporated or adapted to their work. These individuals are the innovators or early adopters (Rogers, 1995). In the middle are the early and late majority: those who adopt technology if they can be convinced it is worthwhile or if it merely replaces something they already do but helps them do it more effectively or efficiently. An example is the individual who obtains a PDA because she or he already keeps a calendar, a to-do list, and an address book. When this person converts to using a PDA, she or he then has access to what else the PDA can provide. It can then be extended to other work in an office or department. Finally, there are the laggards (Rogers, 1995), those who are comfortable with the technology they have but come to realize that by not adopting some newer form of technology they are in danger of being left out or left behind. An example is the people who finally activated their university e-mail accounts because enough administrative offices ceased to distribute hard copies of announcements and the only way for them to obtain the information was via e-mail.

One's attitude toward the adoption of and use of technology has an impact on one's ability to critically engage with the technology. Those at the innovation end of this spectrum may have difficulty being critical in their assessment of technology. In many cases, these individuals operate from the "technology is good" mindset. If it is new, then it should be used; negative by-products may be ignored or missed. Those at the other end resist engaging with technology, so they are not in the position to assess any particular technological innovation's value and worth. These individuals tend to operate from the "technology is overblown" (or "evil" or "antistudent") mindset. But those in the middle, the majority, have the perspective to develop the "both-and" critical mindset needed to overcome dualistic thinking about technology.

Adaptability is an important characteristic of the technologically engaged student affairs professional. It involves the expectation of change, the anticipation of change, and the acceptance of change as a normal way of doing business. In the mid-1990s the Web was new, interesting, and separate from most of student affairs. Today, there is hardly a student affairs department or program that is not using some aspect of the Internet. With regard to technology, adaptability means being willing to learn new skills, change the tasks of one's job, and take responsibility for incorporating technology into one's job in order to better meet the needs of students.

A major technology-related dualism is that there are people persons and technology persons (that is, techies). The perception is that there are those staff who are comfortable with people and those who are comfortable with objects; those who prefer to accomplish objectives through people and those who prefer to accomplish objectives through machines and inanimate objects. This is a socially constructed dualism like all the others discussed in this book. At an extreme, maintaining the dualism is an excuse by those in student affairs who perceive themselves to be "people persons" to both avoid dealing with technology and to see their more technologically involved colleagues as somehow not one of "us"—the "real" student affairs types. This dualism must be transcended. However, the fact that it is a socially constructed dualism does not make it any less real in its ability to divide an organization. The technology side of administration has developed its own language (for example, ISP, portals,

ROI, URL, LMS). On the one hand, a way to breach the divide is to encourage techies to stop talking "tech-speak." On the other hand, the less technologically inclined staff must be assertive enough to stop conversations and ask for translations of vague words or unintelligible acronyms. Language separates and creates boundaries between those who know and those who do not. The technologically competent student affairs professionals must act as translators for those who wish to be technologically engaged. The act of translation itself engages others. Even the most people-person individual in a department uses technology, whether it is e-mail, calendaring software, SIS, or a telephone. To claim that one is a people person and not a tech person is the equivalent of an individual who says, "I am not good with machines," yet who drives a car. Such a person is blind to the fact that a car is a machine. One need not be able to tell a head gasket from a master cylinder to determine whether a car is useful in day-to-day life.

The trend of techies delivering hardware and software to departments, programs, or divisions and telling others how to use it must be eliminated. The sophistication of most technology has reached a point where it can be shaped to meet the needs and expectations of the end users. The important action on the part of student affairs professionals regarding technology is to be involved in the conversations on campus where decisions about technology applications are made. The needs and desires of end users must be voiced in these campus discussions. Web sites need to be shaped to the expectations of the staff to enhance student service. Administrative software must be designed or purchased with students and staff input. Individual student affairs professionals do not have to know how to create Web sites. However, they should be discovering how students use Web sites related to their office's services, just as one does not need to know how a car runs yet knows what one needs to use it for, whether for transporting groups of children, hauling materials, or performing well at high speeds. The tendency is for the typical people-oriented student affairs professionals to leave technology decisions to techies. This tendency is inappropriate and ultimately damaging to an individual office's ability to serve its students.

Developing a mindset of critical engagement is necessary to becoming a technological artist. Actions of such an artist include partnering with technology people, closing the technology gap, and assessing personal technology use.

## Partnering with Technology People

One way to shape technology is to partner with the technology people on campuses. Professionals must not be passive recipients of technology, they must be engaged with the conversations, committees, and policy-making process related to technology on campus. An example of encouraging a passive or recipient mode relative to technology (rather than a critically engaged mode) is the list of technical competencies from the Association for Counselor Education Students (ACES) that counselor education students should be able to demonstrate before entering full-time employment as counselors. They are (http://www.acesonline.net/competencies.htm)

1. Be able to use productivity software to develop Web pages, group presentations, letters, and reports.
2. Be able to use such audiovisual equipment as video recorders, audio recorders, projection equipment, video conferencing equipment, and playback units.
3. Be able to use computerized statistical packages.
4. Be able to use computerized testing, diagnostic, and career decision-making programs with clients.
5. Be able to use e-mail.
6. Be able to help clients search for various types of counseling-related information via the Internet, including information about careers, employment opportunities, educational and training opportunities, financial assistance and scholarships, treatment procedures, and social and personal information.

7. Be able to subscribe, participate in, and sign off counseling-related listservs.

8. Be able to access and use counseling-related CD-ROM databases.

9. Be knowledgeable of the legal and ethical codes that relate to counseling services via the Internet.

10. Be knowledgeable of the strengths and weaknesses of counseling services provided via the Internet.

11. Be able to use the Internet for finding and using continuing education opportunities in counseling.

12. Be able to evaluate the quality of Internet information.

There is nothing in this list of competencies about engaging with technology professionals to shape the emerging and evolving technologies to the needs of the counselor, the client, or the counseling relationship. Instead, it encourages a recipient mindset, rather than a critically engaged mindset. This must change if technology is to be shaped as a tool for serving students.

## Closing the Technology Gap

The gap must be closed between those in student affairs perceived as techies and those perceived as people persons, and between the technologically literate and the technologically phobic or resistant. Expectations for technological engagement must be made clear, yet those with the power to assert such expectations (that is, those at the top of the traditional hierarchy) are often the least engaged (Moneta, 1997). Students and younger staff tend to be the most engaged with the latest technological innovations. This turns the traditional learning and leading paradigm on its head. This is where pervasive leadership becomes vital. Students and younger staff members must teach and provide leadership to more experienced staff members about emerging technology and possible applications and innovations. For example, in student activities at Lynchburg College, students set up an instant messaging program on the director's computer because they preferred that to receiving e-mail. Divisions of student affairs with a culture of pervasive leadership who seek to shape their practice through assessment will be more able to take advantage of the skills and abilities of cutting-edge aspects of technology.

## Personal Assessment of Technology Use

A technology mindset is not just about thinking about what new technology can be used to further enhance work; it is integrated with an assessment mindset that considers how technology is shaping behavior. E-mail is one example; however, the idea of assessing impact can and should be applied to other forms of technology as well. No one can argue against the positive aspects of e-mail. It is reliable, efficient, and allows for quick communication and rapid reply. It also has its well-known downside of replies to a group or listserv when the message was meant for an individual, and misunderstanding and misinterpretation by the receiver given the lack of nonverbal content. E-mail has an urgency about it, not unlike receiving a package from Federal Express—it must be opened immediately. For some, each time an e-mail message is received while logged onto their computer, they are notified. Few people read e-mail only once per day, the way snail mail is read. Going back to Farson's (1996) argument that technology shapes the user, it is important for professionals to assess how technology is shaping their behavior and to become present to and conscious of this process. She or he then is able to make choices in line with her or his priorities, values, and principles. So, back to the example, student affairs professionals need to be cognizant of how they use e-mail. The questions must be both, How does e-mail improve communication? and How does e-mail impede communication? E-mail is great for simple communications such as scheduling gatherings with multiple parties and for sharing information efficiently across campus and beyond. But it is far less effective as a medium for discussion and for solving problems. How many times have there been "dueling e-mails" or "e-mail wars"? An informal rule in place at one institution is that if something takes more than two e-mails, it is too complex for this medium and a telephone call or meeting is needed. Technology tools and media need to be assessed.

---

Technology will continue to be a dominant influence in the planning and practice of student affairs. As indicated in this chapter, student affairs professionals must see technology as both a tool to use in their work and as a medium through which they accomplish their work. They also need to recognize that these tools and media shape them and their work in an ongoing fashion. Professionals should become aware of the role that technology plays in their daily work lives and its influence on how they do their work, what they focus on, and how it shapes their interactions with students and other staff. Only by becoming aware can people take a more active role in choosing the appropriate tools to do their work, shape technology to meet their needs, and be more intentional about technology-related decisions and the impact of such decisions on their work and students.

# Part III

# Seeing Beyond the Horizon
## *Emerging Competencies*

Part Three goes beyond rethinking current student affairs practice. It presents two emerging competencies that are suggested by the interaction of a new science perspective with current events and issues being addressed by student affairs professionals.

Chapter Seven, "Adopting a Global Perspective," arises from both the awareness of the increasing interconnectedness between American higher education and society and the rest of the world and recent events that have shattered the illusion of American detachment from the world (for example, 9/11, severe acute respiratory syndrome [SARS]). Adopting a global perspective includes incorporating international and intercultural dimensions into postsecondary teaching, research, administration, and service functions. The chapter delineates aspects of a global perspective and suggests activities for developing such a perspective.

Chapter Eight, "Futures Forecasting," presents an emergent competency that focuses on influencing and shaping the future into which student affairs professionals, institutions, and the field of student affairs is now living. One of the paradoxes presented in this volume is that although the new science shatters the illusion of predicting the future, considering and consciously shaping the future becomes all the more important. Futures forecasting is the study of the future for the purpose of making decisions and taking action today that will influence the creation of the future. The chapter describes the mindset needed for futures forecasting and presents techniques and methods of the practice of futures forecasting.

# 7

# Adopting a Global Perspective

The internationalization of American society and higher education has accelerated in this still young century. Technology, telecommunications, and transportation have rendered many borders and boundaries irrelevant. Countries, economies, cultures, and societies grow more inextricably interconnected each day. The terrorist attacks of September 11, 2001 shattered Americans' perceived distance from and immunity to world events. U.S. civilians who, for the most part, perceived themselves as spectators of global conflict became participants that day. Student affairs professionals, as well, need to fully and consciously participate in global issues. This is referred to as adopting a global perspective and is an important and emerging competency of this new century in the work of student affairs. The notion of adopting a global perspective involves the incorporation of international and intercultural dimensions into teaching, research, administration, and service functions (de Wit, 2002). In this chapter, the terms *globalization* and *internationalization* are used synonymously.

It was not just 9/11 that brought global issues to American society and higher education. Woodard, Love, and Komives (2000) described some of the societal trends and change drivers shaping higher education and student affairs at the beginning of this new century, including technology, diversity, accountability, rising costs and shifting funding sources, and the impact of the marketplace.

Their list also included globalization—economic, financial, technological, political, sociocultural, and educational globalization. National economies have grown increasingly interconnected. Technology continues to shrink distances and dissolve barriers between countries and continents. Diverse cultures are interacting with both positive and negative results. Considering the events of 9/11 and its aftermath, one can see all of these issues at play.

Even when looking "just" at the United States, the increasing diversification of the population—both through differential birth rates of whites and people of color and through immigration—is making American society truly multicultural and connected with regions and societies beyond national borders (Hanson & Meyerson, 1995). By the middle of this century, the white population of the country will lose its majority status, dropping below 50 percent of the overall population, thus becoming one of many "minorities" in American society. This has already occurred in several states.

Also, for most of its history, higher education in the United States (except for community colleges and proprietary institutions) has operated as though it existed outside the influence of the economic marketplace. This is no longer the case, and the marketplace has grown increasingly global with the lowering of trade barriers and the proliferation of more open economies. Institutions are seeking revenues elsewhere as state and federal support of higher education declines, as well as seeking partnerships with corporate entities here and abroad. Ultimately, it appears that the world is becoming a single marketplace of ideas, information, knowledge, and communication. Then-President Clinton (White House, 2000) underscored the priority of an international focus and the importance of higher education in that effort in a memorandum to heads of federal departments and agencies:

> To continue to compete successfully in the global economy and to maintain our role as a world leader, the United States needs to ensure that its citizens develop a broad understanding of the world, proficiency in other

languages, and knowledge of other cultures. America's leadership also depends on building ties with those who will guide the political, cultural, and economic development of their countries in the future. A coherent and coordinated international education strategy will help us meet the twin challenges of preparing our citizens for a global environment while continuing to attract and educate future leaders from abroad.

Higher education has been and continues to be a significant point of interaction between the United States and the rest of the world. More than a half million international students studied in the United States in 2000–2001, with little or no change in the immediate aftermath of the terrorist attacks of September 11, 2001 (Hey-Kyung, 2001). In fact, de Wit (2002) describes a transition from international education (education about international issues) to the internationalization of higher education, whereby American higher education is increasingly linked to other societies and regions and the core functions of the university—especially knowledge generation—are becoming more globalized. During the 1990s, the European Union and the United States discussed programs whose objectives included improving transatlantic student mobility (including portability of academic credits and diplomas), exchanging expertise in new development in higher education and vocational training, and forming or enhancing partnerships among higher education institutions and professional organizations (Englesson, 1995). Altbach (2001) points out that the World Trade Organization (WTO) has included higher education as one of the products under its purview, so the boundaries between American higher education and the higher education systems of other countries is slowly eroding as well.

Boundaries are permeable—an attribute of an open systems view of the world—and growing more so. Information is flowing freely to and from most countries. Yet as the attacks of 9/11 also make clear, there are chasms of difference that still exist throughout the world, and these differences are coming into greater contact and conflict with one another. Great misunderstandings and hostility exist that significantly influence and alter the world. Yet although clearly an important issue to understand and address even before the events of 9/11, student affairs has been, for the most part, oblivious to the issues of globalization and the potential impact of globalization on higher education, students, and the role of student affairs. Love and Yousey (2001) analyzed student affairs "texts" from 1999 with the purpose of discovering on what issues student affairs professionals were spending time and saw as important. The texts they analyzed included Web sites, newsletters, periodicals, and conference programs from national, regional, and state organizations. They looked at material from general student affairs organizations, such as the American College Personnel Association (ACPA) and the National Association of Student Personnel Administrators (NASPA), as well as functional area organizations focusing on areas such as residence life, student activities, college unions, new student orientation, and Greek affairs. One disturbing finding was the almost total lack of focus in student affairs on issues of globalization and the internationalization of higher education. Of the more than 1,100 analysis units identified in student affairs texts, only twelve of them focused on international education, and most of those dealt with the issue of international students on American campuses. In fact, Love and Yousey discovered a related theme in their discourse analysis—the virtual absence of an external focus. For example, they discovered only a very small focus on the impact of distance learning on student affairs work, and no evidence of student affairs professionals engaging in institutional or transinstitutional discussions related to the implementation of distance learning and its impact on issues of holistic student learning and development. Distance education is apparently considered beyond the responsibility of student affairs. There was also virtually no discussion of collaboration or partnerships with other institutions or with external agents, such as businesses, governmental agencies, or organizations in the growing for-profit higher education industry. For a field supposedly dominated by extroverts, student affairs professionals as a group appear to be very internally focused. An implication of these findings related to adopting a global perspective is that this competency currently runs counter to a strong aspect of the overall culture of student affairs.

Other evidence exists for the lack of attention paid to the issue of globalization and international dimensions of higher education. A report from ACPA, *Higher Education Trends for the Next Century: A Research Agenda for Student Success* (Johnson & Cheatham, 1999), fails to mention globalization as a trend worthy of the field's focus or as a research emphasis. Given the focus on globalization and internationalization in documents identifying societal and higher education trends that were noted in Woodard, et al. (2000), it is quite surprising that the ACPA document would make no mention of international issues, especially since European institutions of higher education have been bringing student affairs professionals to their countries to assist them in the process of professionalizing their student service operations since the mid-1990s. One would think this is a growing trend and worth considering as a focus of both research and practice. Yet in fairness, it is not surprising that student affairs discourse fails to be focused on global issues. American society exhibits a passive isolationism reinforced by the media, media who provide news segments entitled "World in a Minute." So as members of this society, it is not a surprise that student affairs professionals have lacked a global focus. But in this new world student affairs must lead and not follow.

## Defining and Describing a Global Perspective

Multicultural competence has been an important focus in the field for many years and an issue with which professionals continue to struggle. The competency of adopting a global perspective flows from this traditional competency, and is synonymous with the concepts of international, transnational, and intercultural perspectives (Institute of International Education, 1997). Merryfield (1995) includes having cross-cultural understanding, being open-minded, appreciating complexity, resisting stereotyping, and recognizing, acknowledging, and appreciating other peoples' points of view as important in the development of a global perspective.

A global perspective for the individual professional involves:

1. Perceiving the world as a system and recognizing the interdependency of the nations, societies, and cultures of the world

2. Recognizing that what is done and decided here in the United States has implications for what happens elsewhere (and vice versa)

3. Perceiving oneself as a global citizen, as well as an American citizen

4. Being aware of and using multiple and divergent perspectives when addressing events and issues

5. Recognizing the interconnectedness of ecological, cultural, social, economic, political, and technological systems

6. Recognizing and appreciating differences in value, belief, and meaning systems and cultural patterns

7. Seeing things through the eyes, minds, and experiences of others within and beyond national boundaries (that is, perspective taking)

8. Seeking knowledge of experiences, conflicts, challenges, and events occurring beyond the physical borders of the United States and reflecting on and discovering their implications here

9. Seeking peace, positive citizenship, human dignity, human rights, self-determination, and social justice here and internationally

10. Seeking understanding of the factors and underlying causes that surround poverty, injustice, inhumanity, conflict, and environmental degradation, both in the United States and internationally

So many of these elements—systems, interdependence, perceptions, perspective taking, interconnectedness, diversity—reflect a new science of understanding and the need to perceive the complexity of the world. To adopt a global perspective means to see the complexity of the world, and being able to perceive complexity makes adopting a global perspective almost inevitable. Adopting a global perspective also means encouraging one's staff and students to see the world from a global perspective (Williamson, 2002).

Adopting a global perspective may not appear, in many cases, to have an immediate and visible impact on the work done on a day-to-day basis. For other than those working directly with international students, international events and issues are considered, if they are considered at all, beyond the horizon of the immediate work of student affairs. Certainly, as one actively reflects on, adopts, and integrates a global perspective into one's work, issues of planning and organizing are affected. More is taken into consideration. Opportunities for considering potential global impacts of campus decisions and for considering campus impacts of global events become more apparent (Williamson, 2002).

There are many dimensions to adopting a global perspective; however, two basic and integrated dimensions are (1) working with American students to prepare them for an increasingly internationalized world, and (2) working with international students and adapting our campuses to meet the needs of international students. An important task for student affairs educators in adopting a global perspective is the role of preparing American students to live and work in an increasingly interdependent and internationalized world—to have them perceive themselves as global citizens. The more students perceive their world from a global as opposed to a regional or parochial perspective, the greater the opportunity for creating inclusive and welcoming communities on American campuses. Meeting the needs of international students includes encouraging cultural sensitivity among staff and students, providing appropriate worship and meditation areas, addressing food preparation needs, and helping international students get linked to the campus and local communities (Barlow, 1999).

When one adopts a global perspective, incidents are seen in a broader perspective and professionals have an increased sensitivity to the impact of external and international events on their campuses and with their students. Dalton (1999) points out that the downturn of the Asian financial markets in 1998 caused significant problems for Asian students studying at American institutions of higher education. There was the need to grasp familial responsibilities that are part of some Asian and Hispanic cultures. The students were here studying to earn and support their entire families, because it took the support of the entire family to get them here. Student affairs leaders had to be sensitive to the situations these students faced. More recent examples had to do with addressing the needs of Arab and Muslim students and the hostilities they faced in the aftermath of 9/11, as well as addressing the implications of the worldwide spread of SARS. The policymaking that occurred in the aftermath of 9/11 also points to the need for better coordination and connection among student affairs units with regard to international students (e.g., admissions, financial aid, registrar, advising) in light of stricter reporting regulations.

## Developing a Global Perspective

Adopting and developing a global perspective requires time, commitment, perseverance, and open-mindedness. It requires active reflection on the elements listed above, and it requires active exploration of the issues underlying the elements of the global perspective. Most of all, it requires actively adopting a perspective that is counter to the prevailing culture of student affairs. Acting counterculturally is a tiring and draining experience, because one is not only trying to change oneself and meeting internal resistance, but one will inevitably be trying to change the cultural milieu within which one works and will experience resistance from there as well. Green (2002) indicates that institutions most successful in internationalizing the undergraduate experience have done so intentionally and comprehensively, have strong leadership at the top, enjoy widespread faculty engagement, and have cultivated an ethos of internationalization. Developing and adopting a global perspective on such a campus is almost inevitable. Unfortunately, few of those campuses exist.

The most effective way for an individual to adopt a global perspective is to travel internationally, spend time in countries and with people native to those countries, and reflect on that experience. However, not everyone has the resources to conduct such travel, so the following suggestions begin with those that can be accomplished by individuals on their own campus. These include seeking non-American perspectives, building relationships with international students and professors, developing relationships with international cyberpartners, using professional associations, and conducting research. They are followed by actions that require cooperation with others on campus or greater investments of time and resources, including learning a foreign language and studying abroad.

## Seek Non-American Perspectives

Perhaps the first step to adopting a global perspective is to recognize that no matter how broadly a person might believe she or he thinks, if one's view of the world is limited to what is seen and heard in the United States, then when compared to the multiplicity of perspectives that exist in the world it will still be rather narrow. An easy way to find non-American alternative and divergent perspectives is to go on the Internet and surf European, African, Middle Eastern, and Asian English-language newspapers and news sites. Also, international newspapers are often available at many research university libraries. One's eyes will be opened to the wide array of perspectives on global issues. One must also be open to reflecting on the defensiveness and resistance that is often experienced when faced with perspectives, beliefs, and ideas that differ so greatly from one's own.

## Build Relationships with International Students and Professors

International students and faculty are wonderful resources for developing a global perspective. From their different societal and cultural perspectives, they have much to share about their own countries and much to share about their observations of American culture. Like any other relationship, but even more so, relationships with international students and faculty must be built on a foundation of openness, trust, and genuineness. Many international students keep their opinions and observations about their experience in the United States to themselves, because they have learned that it is very easy for Americans to get defensive about what others observe about the American world.

## Develop a Relationship with an International Cyberpartner in Student Affairs

A cyberpartner is the modern day equivalent of a pen pal. In this case, it involves finding a colleague at an institution in another part of the world and entering into a relationship of mutual communication and learning. Although it is possible to identify people from institutional Web sites or professional organizations, there may be colleagues at a study abroad site or alumni or alumnae living in the country of interest who can make the initial contact. Although there is not a field or profession of student affairs in many countries, there are still individuals doing much of the work being done here. Connect with them, participate in a mutual exchange of information, and contribute to the further dissolution of boundaries and barriers. There will be language barriers in many cases, but for good or ill, English is an international language and many non-English-speaking countries and institutions have parts of their Web sites in English. Student affairs professionals also can seek cyberpartners at non-English-speaking universities. To accomplish this one will need to enter into partnerships with international students or faculty on one's own campus who speak the language of the country of interest. These people can act as a bridge and translator as one searches for student affairs related connections in other countries. Working together to locate and communicate with such a cyberpartner will bring international students and campus staff closer together and may result in multiple connections with people throughout the world. Finally, once an individual relationship is established, the opportunity to create international partnerships between programs becomes possible.

## Use Professional Associations to Enhance One's Global Perspective

Many professional organizations are developing international initiatives and programs as part of their service to their members and as part of their national conferences. Attending programs or preconferences on international dimensions of higher education and student affairs is a way of learning more, being challenged, and meeting others who are also interested in global dimensions of higher education and student affairs. There are also organizations whose missions are focused on international issues. These include the Association of International Educators (NAFSA) and the International Association of Student Affairs and Services (IASAS), which is an informal international coalition of student affairs and student service professionals.

## Conduct Research on Global Issues in Student Affairs

Williamson (2002) indicates that very little scholarship has been conducted related to student affairs work and the internationalization of higher education. Scholarship is the root of knowledge, understanding, and wisdom, all of which are necessary for effectively adopting a global perspective. Although research and scholarship efforts are proceeding in other aspects of the internationalization of higher education, what has been published related to student affairs has been anecdotal and exhortative in nature. Student affairs professionals (both faculty and staff) need to initiate and support efforts to conduct research and build models and theories from a global perspective, and to critique and evaluate existing theory in light of a global educational community.

## Learn a Foreign Language

As a group, Americans are woefully incompetent when it comes to speaking languages other than English (Maxwell & Garrett, 2002). This is only reinforced by the fact that English has become, especially in business and commerce, *the* international language. Therefore, the motivation to learn foreign languages does not exist in the United States the way the motivation to learn English exists in other societies. Foreign language enrollments as a percentage of higher education enrollments dropped from 16 percent in the 1960s to less than 8 percent at the start of this decade, and very few of those enrollments are in Asian or Arabic languages (Green, 2002). This is a loss for American society, because a language cannot be learned effectively without an understanding of the culture within which it is spoken. Learning a foreign language will introduce a person to perspectives and worldviews that are different from those experienced in the United States. Working on a college campus provides to most student affairs professionals the opportunity to learn a foreign language at low or no cost.

## Participate in Study Abroad or International Travel

Study abroad and international travel are effective ways to develop a global perspective and cross-cultural appreciation, whose positive outcomes for college students are well documented (Cash, 1993; Gray, Murdock, & Stebbins, 2002; Opper, 1990). Student affairs professionals can participate in study abroad or international travel as well. Many institutions have programs that support or provide assistance for work-related or professional development–related travel to foreign countries. An increasing number of professional associations also have developed resources to help their members in this type of endeavor. Another way to address global perspectives is to encourage the expansion of study abroad opportunities beyond traditional European and Western nations and to encourage the inclusion of higher education and student affairs–related study abroad opportunities in professional preparation programs. For example, since 2000, the New York University College Student Personnel program has sponsored a four-week summer study abroad program in South Africa focusing on international dimensions of higher education.

## Be an Advocate for Global Learning on Campus

Although student affairs professionals do not often have access to or influence on the curriculum development process on campus, there are academically related aspects of student experience they can influence toward a global perspective. For example, individual professionals and service learning programs can work to include international dimensions (for example, to clustered immigrant populations) or international trips as part of service learning experiences. The same has been done for business and management internships (Feldman, Folks, & Turnley, 1998). Student programs and activities can make better use of the international resources on campus, especially in the form of international students and scholars, to bring an international focus to their programming efforts. Student affairs professionals can also advocate for including global learning as an element of the institutional mission and a goal of the institution. Such efforts will bring student affairs professionals into contact with their counterparts in study abroad offices, international student affairs offices, and with staff and faculty in academic units. This will enable them to work toward an institutional ethos focused on internationalization.

---

September 11, 2001 was a devastating wake-up call for all of American society to realize that they are in and of the world, not passive observers of global events. Student affairs professionals also need to heed that wake-up call and come to realize the importance of developing and incorporating a global perspective into their work—their work with students, their work with programs, their work with greater publics, and their work with each other. In a very real sense, lives depend upon it. Recognizing connectedness goes well beyond the borders of the United States. The communities that student affairs professionals are building should include people and ideas from beyond American borders. Paradigm transcendence and both-and sensibilities should include national and international, West and East, North (hemisphere) and South (hemisphere), here and there, and us and them.

# 8

# Futures Forecasting

*You can and should shape your own future; because if you don't someone else surely will.*

Joel Barker, futurist

*No one will thank you for taking care of the present if you have neglected the future.*

Joel Barker, futurist

*The future is imponderable, but worth pondering.*

Anonymous

This book is about the future. It has discussed dismantling the constraints of the past, recognizing present and future challenges, and creating visions of the future into which individuals and organizations will live. It makes sense to end with our eyes and minds focused ahead—not just ahead, but ahead of what is immediately ahead. The increasing complexity, interdependency, and pace of change in the world have rendered traditional beliefs about controlling and predicting the future pointless. Yet the shattering of these beliefs does not leave individuals and organizations powerless. Human choice and intention *have* shaped the future. President John F. Kennedy's proclamation to land a man on the moon changed the pace of technological and medical advancement during the decade of the 1960s. A wide variety of technologies were invented while working to meet that goal, including communications satellites, new plastics and alloys, and advanced computers (Glenn, 1994). No one can control the future, but it can be influenced.

Futures forecasting is the study of the future for the purpose of making decisions and taking action today that will influence the creation of the future. Amara (1991) describes it as the art of the possible (describing paths of possible futures), the science of the probable (examining the likelihood of particular paths), and the politics of the preferable (deciding upon particular paths). Futures forecasting is the study of emergent change and the discovering of the range of possible and desirable futures and how they might evolve (Glenn, 1994). It is questioning the future, and involves questions such as, What else? What if? and So what? Futures forecasting does not "produce completely accurate or complete descriptions of the future, but [it does] help show what is possible, illuminate policy choices, identify and evaluate alternative actions, and, at least to some degree, avoid pitfalls and grasp the opportunities of the future" (Glenn, 1994, p. 4). Futures forecasting is not a science. "It can be thought of as an art in that it is creative and/or as a craft in that it applies knowledge and skill" (Glenn, 1994, p. 5). Like student affairs itself, it is multidisciplinary, drawing information and techniques from multiple sources in the academy.

Futures forecasting is not about predicting. No one even in the business of anticipating such things predicted the attacks of September 11, 2001 or the relatively peaceful breakup of the Soviet Union. And although there were a few macrohistorians who were somewhat accurate about the fall of the Berlin Wall by using the hypothesis that totalitarian systems are more likely to implode whereas democratic systems change more slowly, questions about who predicted the result can be framed differently. Futurists would, instead, suggest asking questions, such as, What are the Berlin walls in our lives, in the world, and in our organizations that need to be broken down? The former approach leads to prediction, the latter to questioning. Although it is impossible to predict major innovations and breakthroughs, another reason that futures forecasting is not about predicting is that the process of futures forecasting itself can influence the range of futures and the possibilities of a particular future emerging. A forecast can be one of the slight variations in initial conditions that can result in significant change at some point in the future. A forecast of greater student activism and unrest may make it less likely if it triggers action on the part of policymakers and campus leaders.

Futures forecasting is also not just about planning, it is not even about strategic planning. Most planning processes focus on problems that exist now, in the present. Planning and strategic planning are important traditional competencies that should be practiced. And although futures forecasting can certainly contribute to the effectiveness of strategic planning, it is not about controlling destinies. Futures forecasting is about taking the themes in this book, applying them to student affairs work, and recognizing that although the future is inherently unpredictable, influence can be exerted on the future that emerges. As Barker (1992) argues, people can consciously shape the future. To neglect the future is to leave the future strictly to the actions of the present that are borne out of the past, and to happenstance. Futures forecasting is about creating and influencing; it is an aspect of pervasive leadership. The purpose of futures forecasting "is to systematically explore, create, and test both possible and desirable future visions" (Glenn, 1994, p. 2). It is designed to help make better decisions in planning processes. In fact, given the increasing complexity and pace of change in organizations and society, futures forecasting can serve to increase lead time between potential future events and current planning (Glenn, 1994).

Futures forecasting was given a tremendous boost after World War II with the advance of computer technology and the ability to process huge volumes of data to extrapolate and analyze a myriad of trends. Quantitative methods included system dynamics, time series forecasts, econometrics, leading indicator analysis, and decision analysis. Many of these analytic procedures were used to make predictions—predictions that invariably were wrong. For no matter how impressive the stack of numbers, the underlying assumptions guiding the analysis were fairly simple and grounded in the old paradigm (for example, linear causality, predictability, control). There was the hope and belief that the key to knowing the future was in extrapolating the present by very rational means.

Many of these processes were based on the principles of analogy and continuity (Komives & Petersen, 1997). The principle of analogy assumes that particular patterns of events are part of a cycle that occurs over time or that one event will proceed in the same way as a similar event. The principle of analogy is a concept left over from the agricultural age, when the perception of time tended to be cyclical (Glenn, 1994), as the seasons, weather patterns, temperature patterns, and such associated with particular times of the year. Komives and Petersen (1997) indicate this principle leads individuals to seek patterns telling them that "*when* something occurs, *then* a predictable outcome results. This when-then cycle helps anticipate possible future scenarios" [emphasis in original] (p. 84). They provide the well-known example that *when* a recession occurs, *then* college enrollments increase. However, one of the problems with the principle of analogy applied to human organizing and behavior is that when such a cycle is identified, changes may be made that disrupt the cycle in unpredictable ways, whereas people in the agricultural age (and now) had no control over the weather or temperature.

The other use of analogy is to compare two situations that are similar in some ways. Using the principle of analogy assumes that the situations are similar in other ways as well (Glenn, 1994). Comparing the spread of one technological advance (for example, cell phones) to other similar technologies (for example, pagers or traditional phones) leads to particular assumptions and predictions about what will happen. Analogies can be quite persuasive, but they differ in the cultural and temporal contexts within which these events are occurring. Whatever the United States may have in common with ancient Rome in terms of growth, dominance, and decline, the differences far outweigh the commonalities. The principle of continuity is a product of the industrial age, when the perception of time was more progressive and linear (Glenn, 1994). This principle assumes that events and issues will continue to develop and progress as they are doing now, an assumption that leads to the related assumption that change occurs incrementally. A recent example was the assumption that after landing on the moon, trips to Mars and other planets would soon follow.

Given the increase in the pace of change and the increase in complexity in our society, in the latter part of the twentieth century futurists came to realize the limitations of Newtonian science based on assumptions of rationality, linearity, objectivity, and control. With the emergence of new sciences such as chaos theory and complexity theory, alternative assumptions and methods were introduced to the process of futures forecasting. Present methods, while incorporating elements of the rational paradigm, seek to include the less measurable—hunches, gut instinct, intuition, imagination, creativity, and emotions. They also incorporate elements of the new sciences—systems, patterns, discontinuities, wholes, and relationships. These emerging methods are based on the assumption that prediction and control are not the goals of futures forecasting, whereas understanding and influence are.

The future will happen. The current present was once a future, and it was either shaped from planned activities and conscious choices, or it "just happened"—the default future. As Barker (1992) argues, unless one thinks about the future, someone else who makes time for the future will, if not control, then certainly define the future instead. Planning, even strategic planning, tends to be rooted in the past. It is a process of saying, This is where we are, what we have, and what we are doing. Where do we want to go and how do we get there? The pull of the past is not unlike the constraints of incremental budgeting—that what is received this year is based on what was received last year: a little more, a little less, or the same.

Futures forecasting certainly regards the past, but is alert to those things occurring in the present already creating the future into which individuals and organizations are living, and with those things in mind it also identifies a possible future that can be created.

## The Mindset for Futures Forecasting

Futures forecasting is a way to approach the world and work. Most specifically it is about seeing the big picture and being able to think divergently. This is the practice of asking, What else? One of the most time-honored and effective methods to both see the big picture and think divergently is to read, and to read widely. Student affairs professionals should be reading not only student affairs and higher education literature, but seeking literature and material from other fields as well. Student affairs is a multidisciplinary field that is influenced by so much of what goes on beyond the permeable boundaries of campuses and the field. Professionals need to read, reflect on what is read, and discuss what is learned with colleagues. As simple as it sounds, reading and discussion must be the foundations of any student affairs futures forecasting effort.

Student affairs is a field of problem solvers; however, the danger of problem solving is to converge on an answer too quickly. Practicing divergent thinking encourages professionals to think of more than one right answer. In general it should be the practice of always looking for the new idea, the alternative approach to something, the anomaly, the outlier, the event or trend that does not quite make sense. Exposing oneself to different perspectives and worldviews is another way of enhancing one's ability to think divergently. Interacting and creating relationships with international students and scholars on campus is certainly one way of encouraging divergent thinking and challenging conventional wisdom.

There are a variety of techniques used in futures forecasting that can encourage divergent thinking. Brainstorming is a long-standing, simple method to encourage a diversity of opinions and ideas. It is typically done in a group setting and involves generating ideas on an issue or topic without comment, criticism, or evaluation. Creative, outlandish ideas are encouraged. Only after an entire list is generated are the items on the list discussed, analyzed, and evaluated. The Delphi technique is another method used in futures forecasting that encourages the discovery of diverse and alternative options to problems and issues. Although its purpose in futures forecasting was to come to a consensus about beliefs about the future and future directions (Lang, 1994), it is shared here primarily due to its ability to generate divergent thinking among members of a group or organization. The technique can be used to generate diverse ideas about questions such as, What impact do you think technology will have on the residence halls? How will student affairs meet the psychosocial needs of distance learning students? What changes can we expect in our student body during the next five years?

The Delphi technique was created with the recognition that group discussions tended to dampen diverse ideas, because they have the tendency of being dominated by one or two individuals, tend to pursue a single train of thought that emerges early in a discussion, and because there is significant pressure on group members to conform, often resulting in a false or premature consensus. Therefore, the Delphi technique is conducted outside of a group setting. In fact, the responses of individual group members are typically kept anonymous. The basic format (which is refined depending on the purpose of the overall process) is that the issue or question of the process is distributed to the participants, who comment in writing openly and broadly on the issues or address the questions (Lang, 1994). This information is collected and compiled by a facilitator or facilitating group. The purpose of the compilation is to maintain the breadth and diversity of response rather than summarizing or condensing. This material is then distributed back to the group members, who are free to comment on any or all of the material, including adding additional ideas prompted by the thoughts of others. This information is then collected and compiled again. Depending on the purpose of the exercise, the material can go through several rounds of comment. It should be noted that this technique can be quite time consuming for the participants and for the facilitators, and this needs to be taken into consideration when designing the exercise for a specific use. Also, depending on the purpose, the facilitators can seek areas of emerging consensus or identify polarities within the body of information that might warrant further elaboration.

## Obstacles to Futures Forecasting

Part of developing the appropriate mindset for futures forecasting is to recognize the challenges, limitations, and dangers inherent in the practice. Failing to account for such influences can result in an ineffective mindset for futures forecasting.

### Mindset of Prediction

Perhaps the greatest danger is slipping into the mindset of prediction. The ideas and scenarios constructed through forecasting activities become predictions that will be proven either right or wrong.

### Influence of Culture

Another danger is failing to recognize the important influence of customs and culture that restrict change and dampen trends, especially those that are counter to the prevailing culture (Schnaars, 1989).

### Bias

There are many challenges to futures forecasting and most of them exist in the form of bias. Schnaars (1989) points out that these include the tendency for forecasters to have an optimistic bias (that is, this will be better in the future than it is today) and be influenced by the Zeitgeist effect, whereby forecasters are restricted by the spirit of the times in which they live. Forecasters with the same data would have constructed different scenarios pre–September 11, 2001 than post–September 11, 2001, given the overall change in the tenor of society. Evans (1982) points out that biases influence every stage of forecasting, and include perceiving patterns in random events, maintaining beliefs in the face of contradictory evidence, and generating forecasts least likely to falsify one's own informal theories. Wachs (1982) identifies the biases of relying on outdated core assumptions and the resistance to following hunches or departing from conventional wisdom. Other biases include overvaluing recent events, relying on illusory correlations, having selective perception, and underestimating uncertainty (Makridakis, 1990). It is not surprising that these biases are most likely to come into play and influence the process of futures forecasting in circumstances of uncertainty and complexity and where strong beliefs are held. This describes most situations of importance facing student affairs professionals. An early step in any futures forecasting process needs to be the surfacing and delineating of biases and assumptions as a method to reduce their influence.

## Techniques and Methods of Futures Forecasting

There are two basic tracks in futures forecasting. The first is attempting to figure out what is emerging now that will become evident and influential in the future, which is also referred to as *exploratory forecasting* (Glenn, 1994). What saplings are growing now that will need to be dealt with when they are trees? The second is shaping the future from the perspective of the present and possible desirable futures, which is labeled *normative forecasting* (Glenn, 1994). What seeds should be planted now and where should they be planted? The activities described are environmental scanning, trend watching, scenario construction, and visioning the future; they are overlapping and interacting and can be used in either type of forecasting. It is difficult, if not impossible, to trend watch if one is unwilling or incapable of seeing the big picture. To create a scenario, one needs to have some idea about the issues emerging, which are obtained through environmental scanning and trend watching.

## Environmental Scanning

Environmental scanning is the systematic review of media (literature, newspapers, Web sites, television, radio, magazines) and other modes of communication and discourse to determine emerging issues (Lang, 1994). These issues can be obstacles, opportunities, or trends because the world and the environment for institutions, organizations, and individuals is increasingly turbulent and uncertain. Lang (1994) argues that a process should be in place that scans for emerging developments. Institutions and departments are open systems with permeable boundaries, exchanging information, energy, and materials with entities beyond those boundaries. This interdependence means that organizations need to be far more sensitive to external factors than they were previously. Thus, factors in the external environment have become as responsible for shaping organizations as internal forces (Lang, 1994). Most professionals typically scan their environment. However, the type of scanning normally done by professionals tends to be passive. What is required for this competency is active, conscious, and intentional environmental scanning. It should also be a regular activity, rather than an activity that is done in reaction to a crisis or event. As a reaction, environmental scanning is usually less than useful for the individual or program. Also, although it is quite possible for individuals to be effective environmental scanners, or for that matter future forecasters, it is much more effective if groups of individuals work together. Scheduling time in staff meetings to discuss events and issues as possible trends and to seek their meaning can be an effective use of time.

Amara (1988) warns against becoming a "vacuum cleaner" (that is, attempting to collect every piece of information perceived in the environment), since information is virtually limitless. This can lead to analysis paralysis—having too much information to be able to make sense of it. Instead, one should construct filters to screen data. There are also sources of potential biases associated specifically with environmental scanning that need to be brought to conscious level, or ameliorated through the use of groups. These include preferences for looking inside a field rather than outside, scanning the present and ignoring the recent past, focusing on periodicals and books and avoiding reports and government documents, and choosing print over nonprint media (Marien, 1991).

Although there are many such filters that can be constructed, what follow are three categories from which to choose: sector, scope, and temporal range.

*Sector*

The sector filter suggests focusing on particular types of environments that exist concurrently in the overall environment. These include sociocultural; technological; popular; economic and business; demographic; government, political, and policy; and education, higher education, and student affairs environments. These are not discrete environments; they overlap, interact, and are mutually shaping. However, the purpose of a filter is to focus the attention of the individual or group who is doing the scanning. Following is a list of sectors and topics within the category to consider or specific issues that emerged in the late 1990s to early 2000s.

> *Sociocultural:* continuing diversification of the national population, differential diversity rates across regions, growing emphasis on shifts in spirituality, values, and attitudes within youth population
>
> *Technological:* distance learning, continuing growth of the Internet, proliferation of cell phones and text messaging, and expectation of universal computer ownership
>
> *Popular:* music, fashion (for example, the role of media's proliferation of the image of the "perfect" self and its impact on student development), television, movies, theater, and art
>
> *Economic and business:* jobless rate, job growth areas, recession and recovery, and industry growth and decline

*Demographic:* differential growth rates, burgeoning elementary and middle school enrollments, aging society (retiree to worker ratio diminishing and impact on social security and other federal programs and priorities), and changes in mental health (for example, the increasing number of college students on psychotropic medication)

*Government, political, and policy:* financial aid, research support emphases, balanced budget requirements, accountability demands, prepaid tuition plans, welfare reform, Higher Education Act reauthorization, post–affirmative action and access to higher education, and fair use copyright law

*Education, student affairs, and higher education:* shifts in curricular emphasis, deferred maintenance, increased service learning, graduate student unionization, adjunct faculty unionization, new approaches to teaching and learning, and for-profit higher education

The program or department within student affairs doing the scanning can decide on which sectors to focus their efforts. Obviously, career services offices are more effective when they know the emerging economic and business issues, and financial aid offices must constantly scan the political and policy arena to be able to anticipate changes and their influence on meeting the financial needs of students. Yet most student affairs programs and departments would do well to expand the sectors on which they focus their typical environmental scanning processes.

*Scope*

*Scope* refers to the reach or breadth of the environmental scan. There are many ways to define scope, but typical categories include internal, local, regional, state, national, multinational, and international. Scope can also refer to the field of student affairs, a subfield in student affairs (for example, residence life), or higher education in general. Different issues may emerge at different levels. Internal environmental scanning is an important, though often passive, activity. Active internal scanning should be included in any formal environmental scanning process, and involves consciously investigating and discussing emergent issues from within the environment of the organization. Different institutions and institutional types are sensitive to different levels of scope. For example, a community college will be very sensitive to local or regional emerging issues, but may not be focused at all on national or international issues. Few institutions or individuals are sensitive enough to global issues. Programs and institutions need to identify in which categories of scope they have strengths in environmental scanning and in which sectors scanning is either weak or absent.

### Temporal Range

Temporal range refers to the relative immediacy of impact of emerging issues. There are those of current or immediate concern to the organization (for example, SARS in 2003), those that are not of immediate concern to the organization but likely to be in the foreseeable future, and those weaker or indistinct issues that may or may not have significant influence on the performance of the organization (Terry, 1977). Issues and events of short-term futures are accessible to those who wish to find them and know where to look. In the technology realm, one can find innovations being developed by exploring Internet technology sites, talking with information technology professionals on campus, reading technologically focused magazines, or attending technology industry conventions. From a political perspective, one can pay attention to the various policies being debated and decided upon in legislatures at the state and national level through sites and publications such as *The Chronicle of Higher Education*.

## Trend Watching: Identification and Analysis

Trend watching emerges from the results of environmental scanning. A trend involves an item of interest or issue that is moving, growing, or declining in a prevailing direction. Trend watching involves tracking topics of interest in media, technology, telecommunications, and business. Media is a powerful source of and influence on trends (Merriam & Makower, 1988). The way that virtually anything is portrayed by television, newspapers, movies, music, radio, and the Internet has the potential of influencing work with students. Naisbitt (1982) popularized the term *megatrend*, which is an item of interest that moves in a prevailing direction but exists across the scope of an industry or society. Trend watching also means focusing on and trying to identify overarching, driving forces that might be affecting trends of a more narrow or proximate scope. Woodard, Love, and Komives (2000) identified such a set of overarching change drivers influencing higher education, including the push for engaged institutions, the focus on enhancing student learning, the emphasis on accountability in higher education, rising costs and shifting funding sources for higher education, the increasing influence of the market on higher education, globalization, technology, and diversity. All of these change drivers are operating at the societal or system level but are influencing work in student affairs.

Trend analysis involves not just identifying trends and their prevailing direction, but also what the outcomes might be if some trends joined with other trends (Chase, 1984). Komives and Petersen (1997) provide the example of considering the impact of one trend (continual restriction of financial aid by the federal government) combining with another one (colleges expecting students to have their own personal computers). They note that this then becomes an access issue for students who have limited economic resources. Trend identification and analysis requires the ability and practice of reading professional literature and viewing campus media in different ways. One cannot just read for content and understanding; one needs to read with the goal of understanding how what is being read fits into what else has been read, heard, seen, or experienced, and with an eye toward identifying the bias and perspective of the author.

A word of caution is in order. A trend is a trend because it is something that is moving in a prevailing direction. The inclination is to formally or informally extrapolate trends, that is, assuming the item in question will continue to grow, maintain, or decline in that particular direction and at that particular rate. That is an example of a rational and old science bias. Trends are not fixed structures. Chaos theory focuses on exploring patterns within fluctuations. Anytime there is a prediction of more than a few years into the future based on a trend extrapolation, one can be almost certain that it is not what will happen. If babies continued to grow at the rate they grow during their first year of life, by the time they are eighteen they would be the size of a battleship. So it is also important to analyze a trend for breakpoints and discontinuities in the trend line (Amara, 1988).

### Scenario Construction

A scenario is a story or model of an expected or a supposed sequence of events. In futures forecasting, it is multiple chronological and detailed histories written into and about the future. Scenario construction was developed by Herman Kahn for the Rand Corporation in the 1950s for the purpose of "thinking the unthinkable" in relation to nuclear conflict and military research. Shell Oil Company is the most often cited example of a corporation using scenario construction to help shape its future. By incorporating the practice into its larger planning process, Shell was able to generate a variety of "unthinkable" future possibilities, such as an Arab oil embargo, and prepare for such possibilities. Such scenarios led Shell to lock in long-term contracts for oil, which helped Shell weather the oil crisis of the 1970s. Glenn (1994, p. 3) points out:

> In the process of writing [scenarios], it becomes clear that no easy transition from the present to the future exists for some developments. This difficulty focused the mind on the important questions to resolve in order to design better policy. It forces us to think about the future and helps identify assumptions to examine and change, if necessary.

Scenario construction begins by asking questions related to possible future events. It can begin by playing "What if?" and asking Barker's (1992) paradigm-shift question, What do I believe is impossible to do in my field, but if it could be done, would fundamentally change my business? Or it can begin by asking the question, What would happen if _____ came to pass? The blank would be filled in with information or issues that emerged from environment scanning or trend analysis. Construction of alternative scenarios permits program or institutional members to consider a number of possible futures, including undesirable ones, and permits planning for the most likely eventualities, but also allows them to be sensitized to and be more ready to respond to the less likely or less palatable possibilities. Scenario construction helps then to create strategy that is robust and functional across a number of different possible futures. By understanding the factors that drive events toward an undesirable future, planners can identify strategies to help avoid or at least ameliorate some of the negative impacts if such an adverse future does emerge.

Scenario construction introduces creativity, intuition, and imagination to the process of futures forecasting. A good scenario asks the reader to suspend disbelief long enough to appreciate the point of view and purpose of the future described. Although some corporations hire novelists and playwrights to assist in writing scenarios around various trends and forecasts, most institutions of higher education have faculty in literature, theater, and the arts who might be willing and able to assist student affairs programs and divisions with the process. Scenario construction includes the consideration of several components, including the problem, the time frame, the forces driving the issue, and the certainties and uncertainties surrounding the issue.

## The Problem

Problems should be drawn from the outcomes of environmental scanning, trend watching, and analysis.

### The Time Frame

Defining and delimiting the time frame is important and will vary with the problem and the unit constructing the scenario. Issues and problems involving physical plant, construction, or other capital projects typically require longer time frames than do problems and issues involving staff and students.

### Driving Forces

Also emerging from the environmental scan are the forces driving and shaping the issue. These can include technological, economic, political, demographic, and social forces. In scenario construction, one typically looks for forces operating at a societal or national scope, although significant local forces can sometimes come into play. The driving forces used in the scenario construction process are influenced by the time frame involved; the longer the time frame, the less likely is one to incorporate local forces (unless one works at a community college or an institution intricately connected to the local community). The individual or team who is constructing the scenarios will require data about the forces involved.

### Certainties and Uncertainties

Once the major driving forces have been identified, they can then be categorized according to the degree to which they are certain (for example, demographic trends) and uncertain (for example, politics). The degree of certainty is often related to the degree to which the various forces can be quantified. Certainty and quantifiability are not related to importance, because politics is perhaps the least certain and least quantifiable of driving forces, yet reauthorization of the Higher Education Act will have very important implications for institutions in every sector of higher education.

Once the problem, the time frame, the driving forces, and the certainties and uncertainties have been identified, various possible "what if?" situations can be generated, elaborated, and written up.

## Visioning the Future

Visioning the future has been included in other chapters, including those on assessment and leadership. The act of visioning involves coming to a palpable sense of what the future can and should be within the context, constraints, and values of those doing the envisioning (Ziegler, 1991). It is the process of utilizing imagination and creativity to invent a vision that others can see and imagine working to construct. Visions are different from goals. They are not only grander, but they call people into the future, into the work of inventing the future, whereas goals are possible specific end points. Vision must lead to the act and action of creation, construction, and invention. It is not just about ideas and knowledge, it is about work and action.

Compelling visions and shared visions are a means of connecting the future with the present and discovering strategy, paths, and actions to move into the future (Ziegler, 1991). Nanus (1992) argues that an attractive, worthwhile, widely shared, and achievable vision of the future is a powerful force propelling an organization toward excellence and long-range success. This is the difference between the mission of the organization and the vision of the organization. The mission is rooted in the past and the present; the vision is rooted in the future. The vision informs the mission and vice versa. Visioning the future is similar to scenario creation in that a possible future is imagined. The difference is that one of the possible futures is selected and a potential road to that future is mapped. Without much thinking, people schedule things in the future. Every time something is added to an appointment calendar, the possibility of a particular future is created. Many of those appointments are kept. Some are postponed or cancelled for a variety of reasons. The question related to futures forecasting is, What is the particular future an organization wishes to schedule for itself?

---

Futures forecasting is a form of storytelling (Michael, 1985). Storytelling is an age-old device through which people have long inspired, influenced, and engaged each other. It is the creation of a possible future that helps make a particular future possible. When engaging in futures forecasting, it should be emphasized that environmental scanning, trend watching, scenario construction, and visioning the future are not discrete processes. Each depends on elements of the other. They have been presented in one logical progression for departments or programs wishing to conduct a full-blown futures forecast, but individuals or groups can do any one of the techniques without doing any of the others, although it will be tough to avoid using aspects of the others. Also, the first and last step of any futures forecast is envisioning the future, that is to have a vision grounded in the values, beliefs, and principles that inspires individuals and drives the organization. It is this vision that directs the decision making about what sectors and scopes to scan, what trends to watch, and which scenarios to construct. It is also the result of these processes.

# 9

# Rethinking Reviewed

## *Mindsets and Actions*

The overriding goal of this book has been to provide a conceptually challenging, yet fundamentally practical book for student affairs professionals. Ultimately, the most practical and useful aspect of the text is the degree to which it encourages cognitively complex practice; that is, administrative actions and behaviors that emanate from an understanding of the world as unpredictable, uncertain, uncontrollable, and chaotic. This conception of the world led to the specific suggestions related to notions such as pervasive leadership, assessment mindset, resource awareness, and futures forecasting. The conceptual framework of valuing dualisms, transcending paradigms (both-and), recognizing connectedness, and embracing paradox forms one set of themes that permeate the arguments and assertions throughout this book. In each chapter, their role in rethinking various aspects of practice has been highlighted. However, there are several other themes and implications that run through the text. These will serve to conclude the text. One, of course, is the theme of "rethinking" that is incorporated into the chapter title. Such rethinking reinforces the argument that to think differently about something results in different or additional actions. Beyond yet related to rethinking are the themes of seeing more, adopting additional mindsets, being intentional, enhancing awareness, and choosing the future. This chapter distinguishes among these themes and provides an overall set of implications for the thinking and action of *Rethinking Student Affairs Practice*. Finally, additional information is provided about the rethinking-student-affairs-practice.com Web site.

## Seeing More

In the first several pages of this book was a picture of a duck or a rabbit, depending on the perspective of the viewer. Then and throughout the book readers were encouraged to see "both"; seeing more than was initially seen. "Seeing more" is a dominant underlying theme of this volume: seeing leadership as more than just hierarchically arranged positions; seeing politics as more than just self-interested actions; seeing assessment as more than just a chore; seeing entrepreneurship as more than just what organizationally independent individuals get to do; and seeing resources as more than just money. Seeing more is a core competency of excellent administrative practice. Seeing more leads to "thinking more;" it is an advanced cognitive skill that includes the ability to accept, live with, respect, even embrace complexity, ambiguity, and contradiction. Seeing more leads to rethinking; rethinking who one is and what one is doing. Seeing more leads to choosing, doing, and acting differently from how one acted before. Seeing more is not just something a person does; it is who the person is. It is both-and, not either-or.

Each of the chapters serves as a portal to seeing more. The conceptually dense first chapter does not necessarily lead individuals to or provide them with the guidance to rethink or re-view their practice. That chapter lays the foundation; it readies the soil. Instead, it is in the specific administrative perspectives and competencies contained in the content chapters that provide easier access to seeing more. Given the interconnectedness of the topics, one can begin with any one of the topics and work through the concepts and implications, a process that will lead to "seeing more" in the domain of that particular chapter (for example, future forecasting) and also will lead into the topics of other chapters, such as leadership or technology. So one of practical implications for the practice of seeing more, as well as for the other themes in this chapter, is to focus on the content chapters and use the lens of the specific topic to see more in one's own job and organization. In addition, there is material on the rethinking-student-affairs-practice.com Web site to assist with applying the concepts to real life.

## Adopting Additional Mindsets

Throughout this book the term "mindset" has been used to describe an approach to various aspects of student affairs work, including assessment mindset, intrapreneurial mindset, resource awareness mindset, technology mindset, and futures forecasting mindset. Readers are encouraged to adopt these mindsets, in addition to those they already have, which means readers are not encouraged to replace existing mindsets. The traditional definition of mindset is a subconscious, fixed filter or disposition that predetermines a person's views and interpretations of and responses to situations. People have multiple, interrelated, nested, and overlapping mindsets through which is created their view of the world and their experience in it. Most of the mindsets people have are invisible to them; they are subconscious. Anything that is subconscious is a part of who a person is, because the individual lacks the ability and perspective to reflect on that issue and make choices about it. From a cognitive development perspective (Kegan, 1994), a subconscious mindset is subject (part of me), not object (outside of me). In other words, we *are* subject and we *have* object. Early adolescents *are* their peer relationships; when something is done to their friends, it is done to them. Later they progress to the point where they *have* relationships, and can then make choices about how to respond to actions done to their friends. Subject is that which cannot be seen because it comprises the individual, who cannot be responsible for or in control of it. Something an individual *has* comes under their conscious control or influence. Some mindsets are developed through and congruent with social norms and practices; these norms and practices form the basis of shared culture. For example, decisions about career direction are influenced by what is culturally appropriate, what is "normal." Due to cultural and social influences, men are underrepresented in nursing and women are underrepresented in engineering fields. When individuals and groups become aware of and present to the existence of cultural norms and expectations then conscious choices can be made about whether or not to follow these particular norms and practices. For example, a woman choosing to enter nursing rarely has to justify her choice of career. "I always wanted to be a nurse" is accepted as a legitimate reason. However, most women entering engineering have made a much more conscious choice due to its non-normative nature. So even if this woman has always seen this as her career path, "I always wanted to be an engineer" is probably not accepted as enough of a reason. She is probably challenged to substantiate it more than the woman choosing nursing. The same holds true for the man who chooses a career in nursing. His choice, too, is non-normative and probably more conscious.

The origin of one's mindsets begins early in life and is particularly influenced by the variety of environments and contexts to which one is exposed. Children's minds have extraordinary elasticity; their cognitive meaning-making structures are dynamic, malleable, and constantly self-organizing to create order from the cacophony of inputs they receive. Children are constantly learning, unlearning, and relearning; they do not have fixed mindsets. Although the potential for continuous and lifelong learning, unlearning, and relearning is recognized and advocated, unfortunately it has been shown that for many people the rate of learning slows over time and structures in thinking, perceiving, and responding can become "set" in multiple domains and many parts of one's life. Such mindsets then serve as filters to prescreen sense data (that is, sights, sounds, touches, smells, tastes). These data are not evaluated; they are merely screened into one's consciousness or they are screened out. Therefore, a great deal of incongruous and conflicting information is screened out by mindsets even before reaching consciousness, hence the ability of mindsets to predetermine views, interpretations, and actions.

By definition, a mindset is also fixed; it is immovable, immobile, and immutable. Some may argue about this aspect of a mindset, because this description of mindsets being fixed and immutable sounds too final, too nondevelopmental. Perhaps mindsets can be elaborated, built upon, and shaped, but to focus attention or energy on such actions would fall short of the aspirations we have for the readers of this book—to rethink their practice. An elaborated or rebuilt mindset does not give an entirely fresh look at a problem or situation; it gives a revised look, an edited look. The new is built onto the old, and everything is still somehow grounded in the old. However, when a person sees a duck, they only see the duck—the duck is one unelaborated, unmelded mindset. In addition, a person who sees a duck will always be able to see a duck. Even if the person comes to see the rabbit—a different, fixed, unelaborated mindset—she or he will also always be able to see the duck. One cannot "unsee" the duck and only see the rabbit. A person raised in a racist environment who develops a racist mindset will always have the choice of viewing the world through that mindset, even if that person comes to develop and adopt an alternate mindset of equity, equality, and embracing of difference. The racist mindset does not disappear, anymore than the duck disappears. A person recovering from racism has multiple ways and, therefore, a much more complex way of viewing racial issues than someone who was raised in a nonracist culture and only developed an equity mindset.

There is a freedom that emerges when time and energy are not spent trying to eliminate or "fix" a particular mindset. This relates to the argument in the assessment chapter about defusing, as opposed to dismantling, obstacles. Instead, energy is better used on seeing more; on consciously adopting additional or alternative mindsets and, other than becoming aware of them, letting the old mindsets be. Our brains have apparently unlimited capacity for thoughts, experiences, ideas, and mindsets, and so old ones do not need to be removed in order to add new and different ones. In addition, from the perspective of student affairs administration and leadership, old mindsets have had their degrees of effectiveness. Practices grounded in Newtonian assumptions have contributed greatly to building organizations and programs that serve the needs of students. The argument in this book is that new mindsets can see better or additional ways of serving the needs of students. So the encouragement is to add additional mindsets, not focus energy on destroying or eliminating old ones. Old mindsets should be allowed to coexist with new mindsets. Learning to "think outside the box" requires another box, but it does not require destroying the old box.

## Awareness and Intentionality

The ability to see more and adopt alternative mindsets requires awareness and intentionality: awareness of current ways of seeing and current mindsets, and intentionality about discovering current ways of seeing and current mindsets and intentionality about seeing more and adopting additional mindsets. It is possible, though unlikely, for awareness of current mindsets to come through chance and serendipity. Experiences occur that cause individuals to reflect on how they view the world, themselves, or their work. This can lead to the discovery of mindsets. Unfortunately, although chance and serendipity is a fine and effective way for children to learn, the range of what constitutes chance and serendipity for most adults is regrettably narrow. This means that potentially ambiguous or contradictory stimuli are not perceived as such. As indicated previously, mindsets both filter in and screen out data, so most incongruous and contradictory data are either screened out before they have the opportunity to be recognized as such or filtered in such a way as to reduce or eliminate the ambiguity or incongruity. Therefore, the opportunity to reflect on knowledge and information that conflicts with one's view of leadership, innovation, or resources is absent. Reflect on the experience of reading this book. Were there arguments made that were readily accepted (that is, they fit an already existing mindset)? Were there assertions that were rejected out of hand as wrong (that is, they contradicted an already existing mindset)? If there were examples of "wrong assertions," how many times were the rejections used as a point of reflection (that is, the possibility of creating an alternative mindset) and how many times were they merely passed over on the way to reading the next point (that is, reinforcing the current mindset)? Finally, how much of the cognitive action implied in this set of questions was less than fully conscious (only now is the process recognized due to being challenged to think about it)? So a first new mindset that needs to be created is a "discovering mindsets" mindset that includes an intentional openness to and search for ambiguous, incongruous, and contradictory information and assertions. As implied above, the information and perspectives discussed in the content chapters provide windows not just to see more, but also to discover current mindsets and form additional mindsets about the topics in question.

A person cannot adopt multiple mindsets in a particular domain (for example, leadership) in a subconscious fashion, because the existence of two (or more) separate mindsets about a particular domain implies that conscious choice is involved in which a mindset is used to drive subsequent thinking, action, and behavior. If there is no conscious choice then an alternate mindset does not exist, since the existing mindset will be the default choice in non-reflective decisions about how to view leadership. What this means is that understanding the content of this book does not ensure or make likely that new mindsets will be developed. Old mindsets are powerful. The information in this book is being filtered through them. Developing and adopting new and additional mindsets requires discovery of existing mindsets (that is, awareness), intentional reflection (rethinking), and intentional practice. Thinking and action are mutually shaping only in the context of conscious awareness. Otherwise it is all interpreted through the default, subconscious mindset.

## Creating the Future Through Choice

The existence of multiple mindsets does not imply that each results in action. Just because someone has a traditional mindset about leadership and adds a mindset that reflects pervasive leadership does not mean that the individual must act on both of these multiple views of the world. Instead, it means they have choice in how they will act; they have a conscious choice in how they will interpret the situation facing them. The mindsets are now conscious and, therefore, *object,* so how a person acts becomes a matter of volition, not habit. As two or more mindsets coexist the individual can choose how to view and perceive a situation. That individual can see both hierarchically arrayed leadership positions and the leadership actions and activities pervading the organization.

An important observation, made in other parts of this book, is to notice where mindsets are located, that is, where they were created and what they represent—the past. This is another example of the past overdetermining an individual's future and, in this case, it is accomplished subconsciously. In simple terms, mindsets determine and shape one's future, because they predetermine what will be seen. So what a person sees in the future is subconsciously determined by a mindset that was created in the past. Adopting additional and conscious mindsets provides the opportunity to shift the determination of the future from the past to the present.

Everything a person does creates the future. The actions taken and not taken now cause ripples of effect into the future. These effects are not linear and are not associated with increasing predictability. Actions taken now join, conflict with, resonate with, and diverge from actions of other people and groups in a nonlinear fashion. Cause and effect (that is, I do A and B happens) in the traditional sense is meaningless when viewed through the perspective of the new science. Still, everything a person does creates the future; it is just that it does so in an unpredictable fashion.

So the final implication of this volume is that seeing more, adopting additional mindsets, enhancing awareness, transcending paradigms, embracing paradoxes, and recognizing connectedness enhance the opportunity and ability of individuals and the organizations in which they work to create their future through the practice of conscious choice. The influence of the past declines and the visions of the future lead to choices made in the present that move individuals and groups in the direction of that chosen future.

## Rethinking-student-affairs-practice.com

As indicated in the Preface to this book, readers are invited to join us in the community of authorship. Like all written material, especially of an intellectual or academic nature, this book is either a work in progress or in the process of decay, hence the need for revised editions of books. Technology allows us to continue the development of the ideas and arguments that we write about in this book. Again, we invite you to participate by visiting the Web site and communicating directly with us and one another.

The Web site is a work in progress as well. We are working with graduate students in student affairs, not professional Web designers (Kristen Lynaugh, a student affairs master's student, was the first Webmaster who brought our conceptual design to cyberspace). As of the publication of this book, the site contains the following sections:

- E-mail link to the authors
- Summary of the contents of each chapter
- Reflection and discussion questions for each chapter
- Exercises, examples, cases, and training materials for each chapter

- Places to post questions, comments, critiques, and suggestions about what we have to say about the topics

- An assessment instrument through which we are collecting structured feedback

- Links to other sites for more information about the topics of the book

- Opportunities to participate in our ongoing work to understand and enhance student affairs practice (for example, through focused discussion groups, research, and so forth)

We thank you for accompanying us on this journey. We look forward to hearing from you and we wish you the very best as you rethink your student affairs practice.

# References

Allen, K. E., & Cherrey, C. (2000). *Systemic leadership: Enriching meaning in our work*. Lanham, MD: University Press of America.

Altbach, P. G. (2001, May 11). Why higher education is not a global commodity. *The Chronicle of Higher Education*. Retrieved from: http://chronicle.com/review.

Altbach, P. G. (2002). Perspectives on international higher education. *Change, 34*(3), 29–31.

Amara, R. (1988). What we have learned about forecasting and planning. *Futures, 20*(4), 385–401.

Amara, R. (1991). Views on futures research methodology. *Futures, 23*(6), 645–649.

American College Personnel Association. (1994). *The student learning imperative: Implications for student affairs*. Washington, DC: Author.

American Council on Education (1949/1994). The student personnel point of view. In A. L. Rentz (Ed.), *Student affairs: A profession's heritage* (pp. 108–123). Lanham, MD: University Press of America.

Angelo, T. A. (1995, November). Reassessing (and defining) assessment. *AAHE Bulletin, 95.*

Argyris, C. (1976). *Increasing leadership effectiveness*. New York: Wiley.

Argyris, C., & Schön, D. (1974). *Theory into practice*. San Francisco: Jossey-Bass.

Argyris, C., & Schön, D. A. (1996). *Organizational learning II: Theory, method, and practice*. Reading, MA: Addison-Wesley.

Astin, A. W., & Astin, H. S. (2000). *Leadership reconsidered: Engaging higher education in social change*. Battle Creek, MI: W. K. Kellogg Foundation.

Baldridge, J. V. (1971). *Power and conflict in the university*. New York: Wiley.

Barker, J. A. (1992). *Future edge: Discovering the new paradigm of success*. New York: Morrow.

217

Barlow, A. R. (1999). Global issues confronting student affairs leaders. In J. C. Dalton (Ed.), *Beyond borders: How international developments are changing student affairs practice* (pp. 53–57). New Directions for Student Services, no. 86. San Francisco: Jossey-Bass.

Barnard, C. (1938). *The functions of the executive*. Cambridge, MA: Harvard University Press.

Barr, M. J., Keating, L. A., & Associates. (1985). *Developing effective student services programs*. San Francisco: Jossey-Bass.

Beder, H. (1984). Interorganizational cooperation: Why and how? In H. Beder (Ed.), *Realizing the potential of interorganizational cooperation*. New Directions for Continuing Education, no. 23. San Francisco: Jossey-Bass.

Bergquist, W. H. (1992). *The four cultures of the academy: Insights and strategies for improving leadership in collegiate organizations*. San Francisco: Jossey-Bass.

Birnbaum, R. (1988). *How colleges work: The cybernetics of academic organization and leadership*. San Francisco: Jossey-Bass.

Birnbaum, R. (2001). *Management fads in higher education: Where they come from, what they do, and why they fail*. San Francisco: Jossey-Bass.

Blanchard, K., & Johnson, S. (1982). *The one minute manager*. New York: Morrow.

Blimling, G. S., & Whitt, E. J. (1999). *Good practice in student affairs: Principles to foster student learning*. San Francisco: Jossey-Bass.

Bolman, L. G., & Deal, T. E. (1997). *Reframing organizations: Artistry, choice, and leadership* (2nd ed.). San Francisco: Jossey-Bass.

Brambach, M. A., & Bumphus, W. G. (1993). The fundamentals of community college fundraising. *Community Colleges Journal, 63*, 14–19.

Breneman, D. W., & Taylor, A. L. (1996). *Strategies for promoting excellence in a time of scarce resources*. New Directions for Higher Education, no. 94. San Francisco: Jossey-Bass.

Briggs, J., & Peat, F. D. (1999). *Seven life lessons of chaos: Spiritual wisdom from the science of change*. New York: HarperPerennial.

Brown, R. D. (1991). Student affairs research on trial. In K. J. Beeler & D. E. Hunter (Eds.), *Puzzles and pieces in wonderland: The promise and practice of student affairs research* (pp. 124–142). Washington, DC: National Association of Student Personnel Administrators.

Carver, J. (2000). Managing your mission: Advice on where to begin. *About Campus: Enriching the Student Learning Experience, 4*(6), 19–23.

Cash, R. W. (1993, May). *Assessment of study-abroad programs using serveys of student participants*. Paper presented at the Annual Forum of the Association for Institutional Research, Chicago, IL. ERIC document no. ED360925.

Chang, P. (2002). N.I.P. (Network/Internet/PDA) those student affairs problems in the bud. *Student Affairs Online, 3*. Retrieved from http://www. studentaffairs.com/ejournal/Summer_2002/NIP.html.

Chase, W. H. (1984). *Issue management: Origins of the future*. Samford, CT: Issue Action Publications.

Council for Aid to Education. (1996). *Voluntary support of education 1996*. New York: Council for Aid to Education.

Covey, S. R. (1989). *The seven habits of highly effective people: Powerful lessons in personal change*. New York: Simon & Schuster.

Cyert, R. M., & March, J. G. (1963). *A behavioral theory of the firm*. Englewood Cliffs, NJ: Prentice Hall.

Dahl, R. A. (1976). *Modern political analysis* (3rd ed.). Englewood Cliffs, NJ: Prentice-Hall.

Dahle, C. (2000, December). Natural leader. *Fast Company*, pp. 268–274.

Dalton, J. C. (1999). The significance of international issues and responsibilities in the contemporary work of student affairs. In J. C. Dalton (Ed.), *Beyond borders: How international developments are changing student affairs practice* (pp. 3–11). New Directions for Student Services, no. 86. San Francisco: Jossey-Bass.

Dennard, L. R. (1996). Leadership and the new science (book review). *Public Administration Review, 56*, 495–499.

Dewey, J. (1980). Contributions to a cyclopedia of education. In J. A. Boydston (Ed.), *The Middle Works, 1899–1924*, vol. 6. Carbondale: Southern Illinois University Press.

de Wit, H. (2002). *Internationalization of higher education in the United States of America and Europe: A historical, comparative, and conceptual analysis*. Westport, CT: Greenwood Press.

Drath, W. H. (1998). Approaching the future of leadership development. In C. D. McCauley, R. S. Mosley, and E. Van Velsor (Eds.), *The center for creative leadership: Handbook of leadership development* (pp. 403–432). San Francisco: Jossey-Bass.

Easton, D. A. (1965). *A framework for political analysis*. Englewood Cliffs, NJ: Prentice-Hall.

Englesson, U. (1995). *Co-operation in higher education and vocational training between the European Community and the United States of America/Canada*. Document of the National Agency for Higher Education on behalf of the Academic Co-operation Association, Högskoleverket National Agency for Higher Education, Stockholm, Sweden.

Estanek, S. M. (1997). *The Institute for Student Affairs at Catholic Colleges: Report of a social action project and contextual essay*. Unpublished doctoral dissertation, The Union Institute, Cincinnati, OH.

Evans, J.S.B.T. (1982). Psychological pitfalls in forecasting. *Futures, 14*(4), 258–265.

Evelyn, J. (2002, March 8). Academic counselors at city colleges of Chicago fear jobs will be eliminated. *Chronicle of Higher Education*. Retrieved from http://chronicle.com/weekly/v48/i26/26a01202.htm.

Farson, R. (1996). *Management of the absurd: Paradoxes of leadership*. New York: Simon and Schuster.

Feldman, D. C., Folks, W. R., & Turnley, W. H. (1998). The socialization of expatriate interns. *Journal of Managerial Issues, 10*(4), 403–418.

Fisher, J. L. (1984). *Power of the presidency*. New York: American Council on Education and Macmillan Publishing Company.

Foundation Center (n.d.). Located at http://www.fdncenter.org.

Freire, P. (1970). *Pedagogy of the oppressed*. New York: Continuum.

Glenn, J. C. (1994). *Introduction to the futures research methodology series*. AC/UNU Millennium Project. Retrieved on December 30, 2002 from http://www.futurovenezuela.org/_curso/1_introd.PDF.

Gordon, S. E., Strode, C. B., & Brady, R. H. (1993). Student affairs and educational fundraising: The first critical step. In M. C. Terrell & J. A. Gold (Eds.), *New roles for educational fundraising and institutional advancement* (pp. 5–15). New Directions for Student Services, no. 63. San Francisco: Jossey-Bass.

Gray, K. S., Murdock, G. K., & Stebbins, C. D. (2002). Assessing study abroad's effect on an international mission. *Change, 34*(3), 45–51.

Green, M. F. (2002). Joining the world: The challenge of internationalizing undergraduate education. *Change, 34*(3), 13–21.

Hanson, K. H., & Meyerson, J. W. (1995). *International challenges to American colleges and universities*. Phoenix: Oryx Press and American Council on Education.

Heifitz, R. A., & Laurie, D. L. (1997). The work of leadership. *Harvard Business Review, 75*(1), 124–134.

Hey-Kyung, K. (Ed.). (2001). *Open doors report on international education exchange*. New York: Institute of International Education.

Iannozzi, M. (2002, July). Planning and fundraising: From bureaucratic to strategic management. *Policy Perspectives*. ERIC document no. ED453699.

Institute of International Education (1997). *Towards transnational competence, rethinking international education: A U.S.-Japan case study*. IIE Research

Report no. 8, prepared by the Task Force for Transnational Competence. New York: Institute of International Education.

Jackson, M. L. (2000). Fund-raising and development. In M. J. Barr & M. K. Desler (Eds.), *The handbook of student affairs administration* (pp. 597–611). San Francisco: Jossey-Bass.

Johnson, C. S., & Cheatham, H. E. (Eds.) (1999). *Higher education trends for the next century: A research agenda for student success*. Washington, DC: American College Personnel Association.

Jones, D. J. (1993). Strategic budgeting. In W. E. Vandament & D. P. Jones (Eds.), *Financial management: Progress and challenges* (pp. 4–16). New Directions for Higher Education, no. 83. San Francisco: Jossey-Bass.

Kegan, R. (1994). *In over our heads: The mental demands of modern life*. Cambridge, MA: Harvard University Press.

Kolb, D. A. (1981). Learning styles and disciplinary differences. In A. W. Chickering (Ed.), *Modern American college: Responding to the new realities of diverse students and a changing society* (pp. 232–255). San Francisco: Jossey-Bass.

Komives, S. R. (2000). Inhabit the gap. *About Campus: Enriching the Student Learning Experience, 5*(5), 31–32.

Komives, S. R., Lucas, N., & McMahon, T. R. (1998). *Exploring leadership: For college students who want to make a difference*. San Francisco: Jossey-Bass.

Komives, S. R., & Petersen, R. J. (1997). Values and principles guiding technology decision making for the future. In C. M. Engstrom & K. W. Kruger (Eds.), *Using technology to promote student learning: Opportunities for today and tomorrow* (pp. 83–95). New Directions for Student Services, no. 78. San Francisco: Jossey-Bass.

Komives, S. R., Woodard, D. B., Jr., and Associates. (1996). *Student services: A handbook for the profession* (3rd ed.). San Francisco: Jossey-Bass.

Kouzes, J. M., & Posner, B. Z. (1995). *The leadership challenge: How to keep getting extraordinary things done in organizations*. San Francisco: Jossey-Bass.

Kuh, G. D., Whitt, E. J., & Shedd, J. D. (1987). *Student affairs work, 2001: A paradigmatic odyssey*. Alexandria, VA: American College Personnel Association.

Kuhn, T. S. (1970). *The structure of scientific revolutions* (2nd ed.). Chicago: University of Chicago Press.

Lang, T. (1994). An overview of four futures methodologies: Delphi, environmental scanning, issues management and emerging issue analysis. *Volume Seven: Occasional Paper Number Seven*. Retrieved on December 29, 2002 from http://www.futures.hawaii.edu/j7/LANG.html.

Larrey, M. F. (2002). Student affairs and academic affairs: Understanding our history and exploring new relationships. In S. M. Estanek (Ed.), *Understanding student affairs at Catholic colleges and universities: A comprehensive resource* (pp. 97–110). Chicago: Sheed & Ward.

Lasswell, H. D. (1936). *Politics: Who gets what, when, and how.* New York: McGraw-Hill.

Love, P. G., & Goodsell Love, A. (1995). *Enhancing student learning: Intellectual, social, and emotional integration.* ASHE-ERIC Higher Education Report no. 4. Washington, DC: School of Education and Human Development, George Washington University.

Love, P. G., & Yousey, K. (2001). Gaps in the conversation: Missing issues in the discourse of the student affairs field. *Journal of College Student Development, 42*(5), 430–445.

Madison, J., Hamilton, A., & Jay, J. (1788/1987). *The federalist papers.* Middlesex, England: Penguin Books.

Makridakis, S. G. (1990). *Forecasting, planning, and strategy for the 21st century.* New York: Free Press.

Marien, M. (1991). Scanning: An imperfect activity in an era of fragmentation and uncertainty. *Futures Research Quarterly, 7*(3), 82–90.

Maxwell, D., & Garrett, N. (2002). Meeting national needs: The challenge to language learning in higher education. *Change, 34*(3), 23–28.

Merriam, J. E., & Makower, J. (1988). *Trend watching.* New York: AMACOM.

Merryfield, M. (1995). *Teacher education in global and international education.* ERIC Clearinghouse on Teaching and Teacher Education, Washington, D.C. ERIC document no. ED384601.

Michael, D. N. (1985). With both feet planted firmly in mid-air: Reflections on thinking about the future. *Futures, 17*(2), 94–103.

Miser, K. M., & Mathias, T. D. (1993). Creating a student affairs institutional advancement program: Strategies for success. In M C. Terrell & J. A. Gold (Eds.), *New roles for educational fundraising and institutional advancement* (pp. 29–40). New Directions for Student Services, no. 63. San Francisco: Jossey-Bass.

Moneta, L. (1997). The integration of technology with the management of student services. In C. McHugh Engstrom & K. W. Kruger (Eds.), *Using technology to promote student learning: Opportunities for today and tomorrow.* New Directions for Student Services, no. 78 (pp. 5–16). San Francisco: Jossey-Bass.

Moore, M., & Delworth, U. (1976). *Training manual for student service program development.* Boulder, CO: Western Interstate Commission for Higher Education.

Naisbitt, J. (1982). *Megatrends: Ten new directions transforming our lives*. New York: Warner Books.

Nanus, B. (1992). *Visionary leadership: Creating a compelling sense of direction for your organization*. San Francisco: Jossey-Bass.

Nicklin, J. (1992, January). Public colleges scoring big in private fundraising. *The Chronicle of Higher Education*. Retrieved from http://chronicle.com/.

Novelli, L. & Taylor, S. (1993). The context for leadership in 21st-century organizations: A role for critical thinking. *American Behavioral Scientist, 37*, 139–147.

O'Hara, K., & Sellen, A. (1997, March). A comparison of reading paper and on-line documents. Technical Report EPC-1997–101. *Proceedings of CHI '97, Human Factors in Computing Systems*, Atlanta, GA.

Opper, S. (1990). *Impacts of study abroad programmes on students and graduates*. Higher Education Policy Series 11, Vol. 2. London: Jessica Kingsley.

Pascarella, E. T., & Whitt, E. J. (1999). Using systematic inquiry to improve performance. In G. S. Blimling & E. J. Whitt (Eds.), *Good practice in student affairs: Principles to foster student learning* (pp. 91–111). San Francisco: Jossey-Bass.

Penney, S. W., & Rose, B. B. (2001). *Dollars for dreams: Student affairs staff as fundraisers*. Washington, DC: National Association of Student Personnel Administrators.

Pike, G. (2000). Rethinking the role of assessment. *About Campus: Enriching the Student Learning Experience, 5*(1), 11–19.

Pinchot, G. III (1985). *Intrapreneuring: Why you don't have to leave the corporation to become an entrepreneur*. New York: Harper & Row.

Pulley, J. L. (2000, March). "Does my million mean anything?" In era of megagifts, colleges try to keep nurturing (and soliciting) donors of lesser means. *The Chronicle of Higher Education*. Retrieved from http://chronicle.com/weekly/v46/i30/30a04201.htm.

Pulley, J. L. (2002, September 27). The vindication of a boring strategy: NYU, mocked for conservative investments in the '90s, shines in a down market. *The Chronicle of Higher Education, 49*(5), A45.

Rentz, A. L. (Ed.). (1994). *Student affairs: A profession's heritage* (American College Personnel Association Media Publication No. 40, 2nd Ed.). Lanham, MD: University Press of America.

Rogers, E. (1995). *Diffusion of innovation* (4th edition). New York: Free Press.

Rost, J. C. (1991). *Leadership for the twenty-first century*. Westport, CT: Greenwood.

Schnaars, S. P. (1989). *Megamistakes: Forecasting and the myth of rapid technological change*. New York: The Free Press.

Schön, D. A. (1987). *Educating the reflective practitioner*. San Francisco: Jossey-Bass.

Schroeder, C. C. (1996). Focus on student learning: An imperative for student affairs. *Journal of College Student Development, 37*, 118–122.

Schuh, J. H. (1990). Current fiscal and budgetary perspectives. In Author (Ed.), *Financial management for student affairs administrators* (pp. 1–19). Alexandria, VA: American College Personnel Association.

Schuh, J. H. (1996). Planning and finance. In S. R. Komives & Woodard, D. B. (Eds.), *Student services: A handbook for the profession* (pp. 458–475). San Francisco: Jossey-Bass.

Schuh, J. H. (2000). Fiscal pressures on higher education and student affairs. In M. J. Barr, M. K. Desler, and Associates (Eds.), *The handbook of student affairs administration* (2nd ed.) (pp. 73–96). San Francisco: Jossey-Bass.

Schuh, J. H., & Upcraft, M. L. (2001). *Assessment practice in student affairs: An applications manual*. San Francisco: Jossey-Bass.

Schuh, J. H., & Whitt, E. J., Eds. (1999). *Creating successful partnerships between academic and student affairs*. New Directions for Student Services, no. 87. San Francisco: Jossey-Bass.

Schwartz, P., & Ogilvy, J. (1979). *The emergent paradigm: Changing patterns of thought and belief*. Menlo Park, CA: Analytical Report: Values and Lifestyles Program.

Scott, R. M. (1996). Using assessment to achieve quality in student affairs. In *Total quality management: Applying its principles to student affairs* (pp. 71–79). New Directions for Student Services, no. 76, San Francisco, CA: Jossey-Bass.

Senge, P. M. (1990). *The fifth discipline: The art and practice of the learning organization*. New York: Currency-Doubleday.

Senge, P. M. (2000). The academy as learning community: Contradiction in terms or realizable future? In A. F. Lucas (Ed.) *Leading academic change: Essential roles for department chairs* (pp. 275–300). San Francisco: Jossey-Bass.

Senge, P. M., Kleiner, A., Roberts, C., Ross, R. B., & Smith, B. J. (1994). *The fifth discipline fieldbook: Strategies and tools for building a learning organization*. New York: Doubleday.

Shay, J. E., Jr. (1993). The president's perspective on student affairs and educational fundraising. In M C. Terrell & J. A. Gold (Eds.), *New roles for educational fundraising and institutional advancement* (pp. 17–28). New Directions for Student Services, no. 63. San Francisco: Jossey-Bass.

Spencer, J. (2000). An assessment tale. *About Campus: Enriching the Student Learning Experience, 5*(1), 13–15.

Sturtevant, W. T. (1997). *The artful journey: Cultivating and soliciting the major gift.* Chicago: Bonus Books.

Terry P. (1977). Mechanisms for environmental scanning. *Long Range Planning,* 10(3), 2–9.

Tushnet, N. C. (1993). *A guide to developing educational partnerships.* Washington, D.C.: Office of Educational Research and Improvement, U.S. Department of Education.

Upcraft, M. L., & Schuh, J. H. (1996). *Assessment in student affairs: A guide for practitioners.* San Francisco: Jossey-Bass.

Upcraft, M. L., Terenzini, P. T., & Kruger, K. (1999). Technology. In C. S. Johnson & H. E. Cheatham (Eds.), *Higher education trends for the next century: A research agenda for student success* (pp. 30–35). Washington, DC: American College Personnel Association.

U.S. Department of Education (1999). *Digest of education statistics.* National Center for Education Statistics, Office of Educational Research and Improvement. Washington, DC: U.S. Department of Education.

Utah Partners in Education (n.d.). Located at http://www.utahpartnership.utah.org.

Vaill, P. B. (1996). *Learning as a way of being: Strategies for survival in a world of permanent white water.* San Francisco: Jossey-Bass.

Wachs, M. (1982). Ethical dilemmas in forecasting for public policy. *Public Administration Review,* 42(6), 562–567.

Warwick, M. (2001). *How to write successful fundraising letters.* San Francisco: Jossey-Bass.

Weick, K. E. (1979). *The social psychology of organizing.* Reading, MA: Addison-Wesley.

Wessel, N.V. (1999, July/August). Run a business like a university? You bet! *Trusteeship,* 29–32.

Wheatley, M. J. (1999). *Leadership and the new science: Discovering order in a chaotic world* (2nd ed.). San Francisco: Berrett-Koehler.

White House (2000). *International education policy: Memorandum for the heads of executive departments and agencies by President Clinton.* Oklahoma City: Office of the Press Secretary.

Whyte, W. H., Jr. (1956). *The organization man.* New York: Simon and Schuster.

Williamson, W. S. (2002, fall). Internationalizing student affairs: Capitalizing on leadership, citizenship, and scholarship. *Michigan Journal of College Student Development.*

Woodard, D. B., Jr., Love, P. G., & Komives, S. R. (2000). *Leadership and management issues for a new century.* New Directions for Student Services, No. 92. San Francisco: Jossey-Bass.

Worthen, B. R., Sanders, J. R., & Fitzpatrick, J. L. (1997). *Program evaluation: Alternative approaches and practical guidelines*. New York: Addison Wesley Longman.

Ziegler, W. (1991). Envisioning the future. *Futures, 23*(5), 516–527.

Zohar, D. (1997). *Rewiring the corporate brain: Using the new science to rethink how we structure and lead organizations*. San Francisco: Berrett-Koehler.

Zohar, D. (1998). What would a quantum organization look like? *Management Review, 87,* 56–58.

# Index